PETER SCHREINER

COACHING YOUTH SOCCER

donated by the

West Vancouver Soccer Club

in memory of

Gayle Fetterley

West Vancouver Memorial Library

**Library of Congress
Cataloging - in - Publication Data**

by Peter Schreiner
    Coaching Youth Soccer

ISBN No. 1-59164-029-6
Lib. of Congress Catalog No. 2002110229
© 2002

Editing
Bryan R. Beaver

Front Cover Photo by
Robyn McNeil

Printed by
DATA REPRODUCTIONS
Auburn, Michigan

Reedswain Publishing
612 Pughtown Road
Spring City, PA 19475
800.331.5191
www.reedswain.com
info@reedswain.com

Table of Contents

Foreword by Jürgen Klinsmann

Dear Soccer Friends,

Housing developments and the automobile have largely put an end to street soccer. The organized coaching provided by clubs and schools has consequently gained in importance. I therefore welcome the appearance of Peter Schreiner's third book, with valuable ideas for coaching young soccer players. With all the attention focused on professional soccer nowadays, many people are unaware that youth coaches are much more important than their professional colleagues. They have to be coach, psychologist, teacher, friend and often father, all rolled into one. They bear a great responsibility for the physical and mental development of the young players in their charge.

Youngsters today are confronted and burdened with more tasks and difficulties than any previous generation. In a media-dominated society, it is increasingly difficult to separate right from wrong. This is why it is important for young players to be able to train in a manner appropriate to their age and to receive an optimal soccer education. Peter Schreiner gives numerous tips from his vast experience of coaching young soccer players. His videos and books have been widely acclaimed, and not just in Germany.

I wish all readers lots of enjoyment

with this book, and especially in translating it into practice on the soccer pitch.

Yours
Jürgen Klinsmann

Acknowledgements

I would like to express my thanks in particular to **Gerd Thissen**, who advised me and was a source of many valuable suggestions on coaching, methods and drills, allowing me to benefit from his/her many years of experience in coaching young soccer players. I would also like to thank **Achim Nohlen**, **Uwe Kiefer** and **Andreas Pallasch** of the German Soccer Academy, who tested new drills and games and made their coaching groups available for the photographs that appear in this book.

Introduction

Are there any "ready-to-use" practice sessions for this seminar?

I am often asked this question by youth coaches who attend my coaching seminars. Why do so many coaches want complete, ready-to-use, practice sessions? Sometimes it is because they are uncertain about their ability to devise suitable practice sessions from what they have learned at the seminar. More often, though, they simply do not have the time to create a suitable coaching plan from the material that is available in a multitude of available books and magazines.

Selected themes

This book presents small groups of practice sessions dealing with selected themes. Most of them contain tried and tested drills, concrete methodical instructions and clear descriptions of what to do. This book does not contain lots of briefly sketched practice sessions. What it does contain is practice sessions which are:
• described in detail, with possible alternatives, in simple language;
• shown graphically, with photos and diagrams;
• and therefore immediately transposable into practice.
This book is intended to be a work of reference. You don't need to read it from front to back. You can simply select a few practice sessions to try out in your next coaching session.

"Appointment" as youth coach

• You were "appointed" as youth coach more or less by chance.
• Your son plays in an under-12 team.
• You played for your club for many years, and after being asked several times you decided you want to help with the coaching of the club's young players. You could no longer refuse to become a youth coach.
• You do not have the time to obtain a coaching license and attend courses.
• You are on the lookout for coaching tips that can be easily and quickly incorporated in your coaching sessions.
In that case you are a typical youth coach, who helps with the coaching of young soccer players for a limited period of time (usually 2 to 3 years).

I hope this book gives you lots of ideas that you can translate into varied soccer coaching specifically aimed at young soccer players.

Coaching Young Soccer Players

Basic Principles

"Coaching for young players is more than just a scaled down version of coaching for adults!"
What does this mean for the organization of coaching sessions and supervision of competitive matches? The following coaching principles take account of the special demands of coaching young soccer players.

Enjoyable and stimulating
For young soccer players, coaching should be an enjoyable and stimulating experience. The drills should be selected to suit their age and stage of development. Explanations should be given in language appropriate to their age group.

Focus on the ball
Kids regard a ball as a challenge. This is why they find drills involving a ball so stimulating and enjoyable. Lots of balls should therefore be available (preferably one for each player), so that each player has as many ball contacts as possible.

No long lines
Young players are very energetic. Coaches should therefore give them lots of opportunities to run around and expend their energy. Explanations should be kept short, so the players do not have to stand around listening. Young players lose their motivation if they are kept waiting in long lines.

Simplified and adapted rules
Beginners need just a few basic rules to play soccer. Nevertheless, it is important that the coach explains these rules very clearly. The coach can also introduce additional rules to reward the players for using the techniques they have learned. For example, a headed goal can count as two normal goals if it is scored during a practice session focused on heading technique.

Organize small teams
Small sided games and drills are tactically easier for young players to grasp, make less exacting demands on their technique, and require each player to contribute to the team performance. The games are thus more intensive and

interesting for each player, as he/she is directly involved in the victory or defeat of the team. Each player has more ball contacts and is actively involved in the game. Another advantage of small teams is that each player has to carry out both defensive and attacking tasks. Even the less gifted players thus have a responsible role within the team.

Limit the size of the playing area

Young players can oversee a smaller pitch more easily. The game situations and patterns of play in attack and defense are easier for the young players to observe and understand. All the moves take place close to goal, so attack and defense continuously alternate and each player has an opportunity to shoot at goal. The size of the pitch should be increased for older players.

Allow everyone to participate

During training sessions, as many young players as possible should be able to play for as long as possible. Young players soon lose their enjoyment and enthusiasm when they have to stand on the sidelines and watch. In addition, the players learn better and faster when they are intensely involved in drills and games. The coach should also allow as many players to participate as possible - and not just the best players - in competitive games against other teams!

Encourage the players to enjoy themselves and experience lots of successes

Individual performance and personal success must be encouraged as much as the success of the team. However, the coach should also remember that in the long term the creativity of individual players can only result in goals and victories for the team if they cooperate with the other members of the team.

Create learning situations that simulate real match situations

Willingness to learn and the desire to perform well are at a maximum when coaching situations are directly related to real matches. Drills should therefore be derived from real games of soccer and made to resemble real match situations as closely as possible.

Select game situations that are typical of soccer matches

The basic principle of a soccer match is: Score goals and prevent goals from being scored. As many drills as possible should be devised with the emphasis on this basic idea, which young players find easy to grasp. Creating scoring opportunities and protecting the goal are the basic requirements, which young players easily translate into practice.

Remember that young players are all different

Coaches should always be aware of the differences in young players' levels of skill, expectations and interests. Young players with different talents, experience and enthusiasm should be allowed to find their own level of play. Some might simply want to enjoy playing soccer, while other might want to learn as much as they can with the aim of becoming a professional soccer player.

Use suitable equipment

A good craftsman needs good tools if he is to carry out his work properly. Similarly, a coach needs good equipment. Young players learn soccer techniques especially well when they don't have to expend a lot of strength. As the demands on their strength increase, their precision suffers. Good results have been achieved with lighter, smaller balls. The young players experience more success moments and make good progress. Coaches also need a lot of coaching aids to make coaching sessions more varied.

Coaching for young players should:

- ensure they engage in lots of different forms of exercise (running, romping, creeping, hopping, climbing and jumping, as well as throwing and kicking balls);
- stimulate learning processes and develop each player's talents to the full;
- ensure that the players experience lots of success moments,
- build up their self-confidence and self-reliance,
- awaken and maintain their enjoyment of soccer.

Communication

How can a coach communicate techniques and tactics, explain drills and ensure that young players learn as much as possible? A number of methods are available:

Demonstrate

A coach does not need to say much. He/she should demonstrate the movements he/she wants the players to carry out, and then ask them to copy him as closely as possible. This is the most economical and rapid way of communicating movements.

Instruct

Clear instructions let young players know exactly what they have to do and leave no room for uncertainty.
Example: "Take the ball and sidefoot it to your partner. The toes of your kicking foot should point outward."

Ask the young players to carry out a variety of movements

To enable young players to try out their own ways of doing things, the coach should ask them to carry out as many different movements as possible, giving them plenty of opportunities to be creative.
Example: "Try to dribble the ball round the cone as fast as possible. Think about how to move the ball in a new direction."

Free play

In free play, young players can try out a variety of movements, new techniques and new solutions to soccer problems. Free play enables them to experiment creatively. If an experiment is not immediately successful, the coach should quietly explain what went wrong. Successes should be rewarded with praise. The players also learn how to get on with other players and to accept the rules of the game and their agreed tasks. The methods of imparting technical and tactical skills complement each other well. The execution of a particular movement may lead on an instruction to carry out a movement first demonstrated by the coach or one of the players.

The players might then play a game to give them the opportunity of trying out what they have learned.

How long does it take the players to master acquired techniques in competitive games?

Motor skills are acquired in three phases

a) The player learns the rough basic sequence of a movement
b) By practicing, and with the help of the coach, the player acquires the fine coordination of the movements
c) A very important (but often neglected) phase is the stabilization and automation of the acquired movement (see warm-up drill)

Months or even years often pass before techniques practiced in training are used in competitive games (league or cup games). Coaches of young soccer players must therefore have a lot of patience.

Structure of the practice sessions

The practice sessions described in this book should serve as a pointer for developing your own practice sessions. The weighting of the different phases and the duration of the phases depend on the objectives of the practice session and the age and development level of the young players.

A practice session usually lasts between 60 and 90 minutes. Each practice session consists of the following phases:

A) Setting the mood/Warm-up games (5 - 10 minutes)
B) Warm-up drill (5 - 10 minutes)
C) Coordination conditioning (5 - 10 minutes)
D) Main phase with focal theme (20 - 30 minutes)
E) End game or competition (20 - 30 minutes)

WARM-UP GAMES

Adult coaching methods should not simply be adapted for young soccer players. For young players, the first purpose of warming up is to get them in the mood. Small sided warm-up games are ideal for this (see pp. 25-52), as young players have a lot of energy and need to keep moving. The coach should therefore give them the chance to let off steam playfully in the first phase of the practice session.

A warm-up program for young players should be designed with the following points in mind:

• Avoid long explanations.
• Start games and drills quickly.
• Warm-up games should have simple rules and demand lots of movement.
• All the players should be involved (no one drops out).
• In warm-up games the pleasure of physical movement is more important than competitiveness. Just playing should be motivation enough - not the desire to win. Games without winners are ideal (e.g. Plague in Venice, Grand Prix and Greetings).

Younger players have very flexible muscles and joints. This flexibility tends to decrease when they enter puberty, unless they follow a special program of exercises. Warming up for under-12s therefore has two main aspects:

• Preparation for learning techniques and coordination while at play.
• Small sided games with or without a competitive character fulfil an important social function and familiarize young players with the sport of soccer. It is not necessary for the younger players to warm up with boring stretch-

ing exercises or classical jogging and running without a ball for the purpose of warming the muscles and thus preventing injuries. As part of their behavior and character training, however, young players should learn as they grow older that warming up is an essential element of practice sessions and preparation for a game.

WARM-UP DRILL

After the first phase, consisting of small sided games, which appeal to the young players' urge to run and play, the players are extremely receptive. Moderately intensive basic movements (e.g. dribbling, feinting and passing sequences), packaged in stimulating drills or games, are one way of achieving the following objectives:

• The players can improve their soccer techniques during warming-up by practicing movements a large number of times until they can perform them automatically.
• Regular repetition of key movements gives the players the necessary confidence to use them in competitive games.
• Practice drills prepare the players for high-intensity drills.
• The time is optimally utilized.

Like a tennis player, who regularly practices important strokes, during warming up soccer players should repeatedly practice the movements they have learned, so that they will become automatic. Depending on the age of the players, the coach should reserve 5 to 10 minutes for the warm-up drill. This does not clash with young players' ideas of soccer training. Experience shows that young players like simple and stimulating practice sequences, which give them a feeling of accomplishment and make long-term success possible.

Warm-up drills should satisfy the following criteria:

• The ball must be an important element, as movement sequences with a ball should become automatic.
• The program should be varied and systematic.

COORDINATION CONDITIONING

After a thorough warming-up phase, the players are ready for intensive drills to improve their general and soccer-specific coordination. This is important for the development of peak performance and should have a permanent place in the coaching of young soccer players.

Coordination conditioning consists of exercises to improve:

• running coordination;
• arm and leg coordination;

- use of soccer techniques while under pressure;
- sprinting and reactions;
- sense of rhythm.

In contrast to the warm-up drill, where the objective is for movements to become automatic, the objective of coordination conditioning is to learn how to apply acquired techniques under difficult conditions (pressure of time, pressure of additional tasks). Practice sessions should also include supplementary coordination drills. The best time for these is the phase after warming up.

MAIN PHASE WITH FOCAL THEME

Each practice session should have a main theme. The main phase is devoted to this theme and if possible it should also be reflected in the other phases. Some of the themes treated in this book are:

- "Feel" for the ball - dribbling
- Juggling
- Taking (controlling) a pass and running with the ball
- Passing - give-and-go
- Heading
- Shooting
- Indoor coaching

The contents of the other phases serve to frame of the main phase. They can be organized variably around the main phase. Coaches can create further practice sessions from the sessions described in this book and adapt them to the player group. They must take account of the players' ages and levels of development and ensure that the demands made on them are neither to easy nor too advanced. A practice session on the theme of "improving dribbling techniques" could contain the following elements:

- a dribbling game;
- a drill to enable the players to perform acquired dribbling techniques automatically;
- coordination conditioning - dribbling with two balls;
- a main theme - learning new techniques or improving and using acquired dribbling techniques;
- an end game or competition: dribblers versus jugglers.

END GAME OR COMPETITION

Every practice session should end with the participants playing freely and competing against each other. The coach must give the players the opportunity to use the techniques they have learned in a competitive setting. He/she should correct mistakes sensitively and encourage the players to use new techniques in one-to-one situations. Creative players need a coach who will allow them to experiment and does not strangle creativity by criticizing and generating fear.

Examples of end games:

- Small sided game (4 against 4 or 8 against 8)
- Tournament or lightning tournament
- Competitions (e.g. burnout or kings and soldiers - see pp. 43-79).

Organization and use of space

Effective and economic planning starts with sensible placing of the equipment and good use of the available space. The space and scarce time should be used as well as possible. Before the players arrive the coach should set up the necessary equipment for the different phases of the session and place within reach any coaching aids that he/she may later need. He/she should mark the pitch for the first game and lay out the coaching aids for the warm-up drill and coordination training. This ensures that the available space is divided up efficiently and the switch from one phase to the next can be made quickly and smoothly. The players do not have to wait around, e.g. during the transition from the warm-up drill to coordination training. Each second of valuable coaching time is used.

Example: Organization of the available space and the practice session

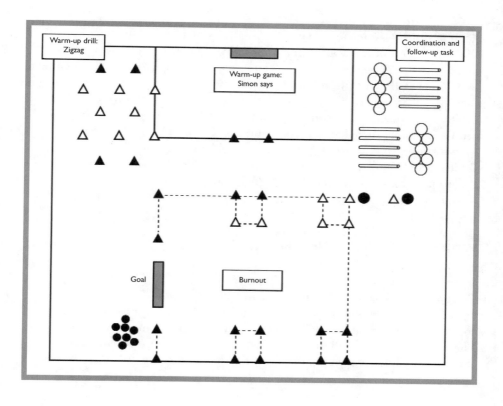

Games for Warming Up and Setting the Mood

Each practice session starts with a warm-up game. This chapter describes a wide range of suitable warm-up games. Select one or two of them for the first phase of the practice session. Young players enjoy some of these games so much that they inevitably want to play them again. Nevertheless, the coach should vary the games constantly to prevent boredom from setting in. Add more games to your collection as time goes by. A good warm-up game can be easily organized and quickly started. The coach should choose a game that is appropriate to the age of the players. "Simon says," "Plague in Venice" and "Fruit salad" are more suited to under-11s, while older age groups prefer games such as "Catch the dribbler," "Burnout" and "Gladiator." The games described in this book can be easily supplemented by similar games.

WARM-UP GAME 1: SIMON SAYS

Game description
The game is played on a pitch measuring 20 x 20 yards. Each player has a ball. The principle of the game is that a command is only carried out if the coach first says "Simon says." The first command is "Simon says dribble!" The players dribble in all directions around the pitch. On the command "Simon says stop," they stop and wait for the next command.

Note
If the coach calls out "Stop," the players continue to dribble, because the words "Simon says" were missing.

List of commands
- "Simon says dribble" (dribble)
- "Simon says stop" (stand still with the ball at your feet)
- "Simon says make a bridge" (bend forward and place both hands on the ball)
- "Simon says hands up" (stand with your hands in the air holding the ball)
- "Simon says circle" (take the ball in a circle round your hips)
- "Simon says feet" (lie on your back and hold the ball against your feet)
The possibilities are endless.

Group variations: "Simon says two feet"

Two players lie next to each other and each holds a ball against his/her feet. The coach can vary the size of the group by varying the number in the command. For example, he/she might say "Simon says five feet." In this case the command has to be carried out in groups of five. Group formation in a game promotes social behavior.

Notes on the method

- The game "Simon says" improves reaction capacity by means of rapid sequences of commands, and improves concentration on acoustic signals and readiness to form continuously changing groups.
- The coach should not explain all the commands at the start, but should demonstrate and name them in sequence. This way the players can remember them more easily. Each new command should be followed by a short practice phase, in which the coach calls out the new commands with and without "Simon says."
- None of the players drop out over the course of a longer practice phase. The fun in this game is that some players carry out a command wrongly and then just lie down instead of continuing to dribble. The players practice the commands and warm up.
- At the end of the game a short competition can be held. Players who carry out a wrong command, or react incorrectly or too slowly, must drop out and carry out an additional task outside the pitch until finally only the winner remains.
- The winner is the player who carries out all commands quickly and correctly until the end.

WARM-UP GAME 2: PLAGUE IN VENICE

Initial remarks

Kids love games of tag. If a coach integrates a game into a story, this introduces an extra dimension. The players adopt roles within a framework. "Plague in Venice" is a game of tag with a simple framework story.

Variation A: Tennis ball

The coach distributes 3 to 5 tennis balls, which represent plague spots. Each player who carries a tennis ball has the plague, and can only be cured by touching another player with the ball. The touched player has to take the ball, thus becoming infected, and must try to infect someone else. As there are lots of bridges in Venice, and the plague cannot cross bridges, uninfected players can save themselves from plague carriers by forming a bridge. The bridge has to stay where it is until a gondolier passes under it, i.e. until a fellow player crawls under it. There are no winners and losers in this game. It comes to an end when the coach sees that the players are losing interest or that the players are becoming tired.

Variation B: Dribbling game

In this variation, played on a pitch measuring 20 x 20 yards, each player has a soccer ball. Uninfected players dribble the ball at their feet. Infected players carry the ball, indicating that they have the plague. An infected player has to touch an uninfected one with the ball to become cured and pass the plague on. The cured player places the ball on the ground and dribbles quickly toward a safe area, while the newly infected player picks up the ball and tries to infect someone else.

Bridge to safety

Pursued players can save themselves by forming a bridge. However, they then have to stay in this position until a gondolier passes under the bridge, i.e. until a player pushes his/her ball under the bridge.

WARM-UP GAME 3: GRAND PRIX

Initial remarks
- This game should first be played without a ball, so that the players can familiarize themselves with the game. It can then be played with a ball as a dribbling game.
- The players learn to cover a short distance at speed in response to an acoustic signal, to stop suddenly with the ball and to change direction to avoid other players.
- The essence of this game is rapid positional change. The coach should therefore urge the players to walk quickly to the middle and call the name of another car manufacturer or "Grand Prix."

Organization

- The coach places cones, caps, rings, mats or any other suitable objects to form a circle. This is important, as it gives the players a target to run to.
- One player stands in the middle and the others stand around the edge of the circle (distance between players 5 to 10 yards, depending on the size of the group).
- Each player has a ball.

Game description

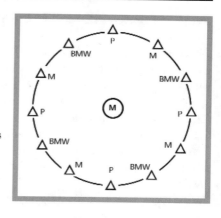

- The coach goes from player to player and gives each one the name of a car, e.g. BMW, Mercedes (M), Porsche (P).
- The player in the middle calls the name of a car or "Grand Prix" and quickly runs to an unoccupied cone.
- On the call "Grand Prix," all the players have to change places. No one may return to his/her initial cone.
- When the name of a car is called out, only the players who have been allocated that particular car leave their cones and run or dribble to another cone. Fast reactions are needed.
- The player who is left without a cone calls out a car name or "Grand Prix". No one drops out.
- To familiarize themselves with the game, the young players should first carry the ball (symbolic of a steering wheel). Grand Prix becomes a dribbling game when the players dribble from cone to cone.

Additional rules for advanced players

The players can only occupy a cone when they have dribbled through the center of the circle. This means that the players have to take more care not to collide with other players.

End of the game

The game ends when the coach sees that the players are losing interest (after 5 minutes).

WARM-UP GAME 4: FRUIT SALAD

Fruit salad is a variation of Grand Prix

- The coach gives the players the names of types of fruit (e.g., bananas, strawberries, apples) instead of car names.
- Each player dribbles to another cone when his/her fruit is called out.
- All the players change places when "fruit salad" is called out.

WARM-UP GAME 5: SHADOW DRIBBLING

- Two players dribble, one behind the other (player and shadow).
- The player in front decides what direction he/she will dribble in and how fast he/she will dribble.
- The player tries to lose his/her shadow by making changes of direction.
- After 1 or 2 minutes the two change roles.

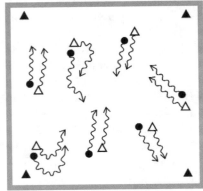

Additional movements
- Stretching exercises with the ball. Between exercises the two players loosen up by dribbling further.
- Feints (dummy step, step-over)
- Turns

WARM-UP GAME 6: CHARACTERISTICS

In most games of tag, the roles are defined in advance. Some of the players are hunters and the others are prey, i.e., they run away. The charm of "Characteristics" is that the roles are defined by the coach's calls. This means that players have to concentrate and to react quickly to acoustic and optical stimuli and signals.

Game description
The players dribble freely around the playing area. The coach calls out a characteristic of a group of players or individual players, who then become hunters.

Useful characteristics
- Color of the players' overvests (e.g., yellow, red, green)
- Hair color
- Color of the players' tee shirts
- First letter of the players' names (e.g., from A to K, L to Z)
- Boys/girls

It is important that the characteristic should be easily understandable. The more general the characteristics are, the more players become hunters. The players then have to concentrate closely on the whole playing area. If the characteristics are very specific, the group of hunters is very small and the players concentrate on the actions of fewer hunters.

Tagged players

Tagged players carry out a task outside the playing area (juggling or dribbling). The game ends when the hunters with the appropriate characteristic
have tagged everyone else, or after an agreed time (e.g. 2 minutes).

Variations:

- *"Characteristics" as a running game*
  The game can first be played without a ball to allow the players to familiarize themselves with it. In this form it is a pure running and reaction
  game.
- *Hunters carry the ball*
  All the players have a ball, but the hunters are given an advantage by
  being allowed to carry the ball. They can therefore change direction faster
  and tag the others more easily. This variant is very suitable for use when
  the given characteristic is very specific and there are thus fewer hunters.
- *The players whose characteristic is called out become the prey*
  The group of players with the chosen characteristic could become the prey
  group. All the other players are then hunters. This rule can be defined in
  advance or can be implemented by calling out the role with the characteristic, e.g. "red - prey" or "green - hunter." This requires more concentration
  from the players, because they have to listen for the characteristic and also
  decide whether they have to run away or chase.
- *Tagged players can be freed again*
  Any untagged player in the prey group can untag a tagged colleague.
  He/she can do this by, for example, simply touching the tagged player. Or
  he/she might play a one-two with the tagged player or play the ball
  through the tagged player's legs. All sorts of variations are possible.
- *Various types of movement can be defined*
  If no ball is used, the players can be asked to hop on one leg, or run on all
  fours, or move sideways like a crab, or run with one hand behind their
  backs. If the game is played with a ball, the coach can specify whether the
  players should dribble with the left or the right foot, or dribble backward,
  or bounce the ball with one hand, or with each hand alternately, or carry
  the ball in both hands, held behind their heads. A typical call from the
  coach might be "First names starting with A to D dribble with the right
  foot."
- *Music*
  If the session takes place indoors, music can be played (radio, cassette
  player, etc.) to accompany the game. The music can be stopped as a signal
  that the coach is going to call out a new characteristic or stop the game
  because everyone has been tagged.

WARM-UP GAME 7: DRIBBLING BY NUMBERS

"Dribbling by numbers" is popular with young players because it requires good soccer technique and rapid orientation on a piece of paper with numbers on it. The number of groups depends on the number of players. A group should not contain more than four players, to ensure that waiting times are not too long.

Material per group
- One ball
- One pen or pencil
- One sheet covered in numbers
  (See opposite page)
- Something to rest the paper on when writing (a piece of cardboard out doors, or any firm surface indoors)

Game description
At a signal from the coach, one player from each group starts to dribble a ball toward the sheet of numbers. The coach can decide the distance that the players have to cover (10 to 20 yards). The first player searches for a "one," strikes it through, and dribbles back to his/her group as fast as possible. On arrival, he/she nominates the next number for the second player (in this case, "two"). The second player dribbles to the sheet and strikes this number through, and so on. The numbers must be struck through in the correct sequence. The coach carries out random checks of this by going from sheet to sheet and checking how far the group has progressed. The group that reaches the highest number in the given time wins.

Variation:
- Two players from each group start together, so that more players are actively involved. The two players cannot start to return to the group until each of them has struck through a number.
- Outdoors the dribbling distance can be greater. In this case the whole group could dribble simultaneously to the sheet. Each player strikes a number through, tells the following player the next number and dribbles back to the starting point. The group cannot set off again to the sheet until everyone is present at the starting point.

Tips:
- The players often cannot find the larger numbers.
- The table function of a PC can be used to create new sheets. The size of the numbers should be continuously changed and the layout of the sheet should be such that the players have to scan it quickly with their eyes.

Typical sheet of numbers

6	24	10	29	16
13	26	37	18	35
21	30	4	32	8
34	19	3	39	25
15	23	12	38	1
31	2	7	20	33
40	14	36	11	27
17	28	5	9	22

WARM-UP GAME 8: ISLAND HOPPING

- Islands (tires, squares of four cones) are spread around the playing area.
- The players dribble the ball freely around the playing area.
- When the coach whistles or calls, the players dribble as fast as they can to the nearest island.
- No more than two players can occupy one island.
- Players who fail to find an island score one minus point.
- The player with the fewest minus points wins.

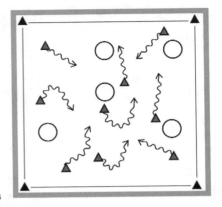

WARM-UP GAME 9: HUNTERS AND HARES

- The players are in a marked playing area.
- 1 to 3 hunters each hold a ball.
- The other players are hares.
- When a hare is hit by a ball, he/she picks it up and becomes a hunter.
- The last hare becomes the next hunter.

Variation:
The hunters have a softball and try to catch all the hares as quickly as possible by hitting them all with the softball. When a hare is hit by the ball, he/she

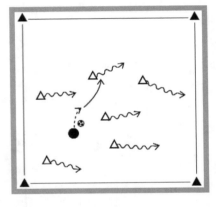

performs a stretching exercise. The other hunters then try to beat the first group's time.

WARM-UP GAME 10: SHIELD THE BALL

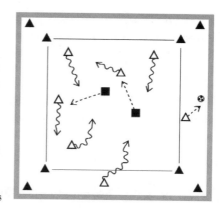

- The players have a ball, with which they dribble around the central zone, shielding the ball from the ball thieves.
- Depending on the number of players in the group, 2 or 3 of them are named as ball thieves. They follow the dribblers and try to kick the ball out of play if the opportunity arises.
- If a player has to leave the central zone to fetch his/her ball, he/she scores one minus point.
- The player with the fewest minus points wins the game.

WARM-UP GAME 11: PICKPOCKET

- The players dribble freely in a playing area measuring, for example, 15 x 15 yards.
- Each players dribbles with a ball and has a cloth (handkerchief, marker band, etc.) tucked into the back of his/her shorts so that most of it hangs free.
- All the players try to "steal" the cloths from the other players.
- They hold the stolen cloths in one hand. If a player's cloth is stolen from the back of his/her shorts, however, he/she has to immediately replace it with one of the cloths held in his/her hand.
- A player can only steal one cloth at a time from another player. He/she has to wait for at least 5 seconds before attempting to steal another cloth from the same player.
- The player who steals the most cloths is the winner.
- The duration of the game depends on the players' motivation and enjoyment (5 minutes).

WARM-UP GAME 12: SIX-DAY RACE

- Groups of two pairs of players (A1-A2; B1-B2; etc.) stand at the start. Each pair has a ball.
- One player from each pair (A1, B1, C1, D1, etc.) dribbles round the playing area.
- The second player waits at the start cone until his/her partner returns. The first player transfers the ball to the second player.

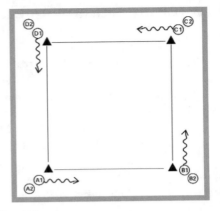

- The players count the number of rounds they dribble in six minutes ("6 days").
- The pair with the most rounds wins.
- Two sessions are played, or a day lasts 2 minutes.

Note
This is a form of interval training, i.e. periods of exertion alternate with periods of rest.

WARM-UP GAME 13: 100-POINTS DRIBBLING

A) Club sport
This game has proved useful as an indoor warm-up game for young players at soccer club level. The coach can use a limited area to provide more than 20 players with stimulating exercise. The players don't just dribble round cones but pursue a joint objective, namely the winning of a competition. The link between the elements of soccer technique and pure chance, i.e. the luck of the dice, is also attractive for performance-oriented club players.

B) School sport
The advantage of this game in schools is the balance between strengths and weaknesses. The element of luck in the throw of a dice gives everyone a chance. All participants are thus equally motivated - boys and girls, older and younger, stronger and weaker players.

Material
Each player has a ball (medicine ball, soccer ball, handball, basketball, volleyball, etc.). Players in the same team can be given different balls, which they swap after each round. The players dribble the ball with hand or foot, depending on which type of ball it is.
- 4 pens or pencils and a sheet of paper on a firm rest (piece of cardboard, etc.)
- 4 dice (preferably foam dice, 4 by 4 inches or bigger, but ordinary dice can also be used)
- Cassette player and a cassette with fast music, if desired

Game description
- The players are organized into 4 groups. One group stands at each corner

of the playing area. All the players initially stand inside the playing area so as not to obstruct the dribblers (see diagram).

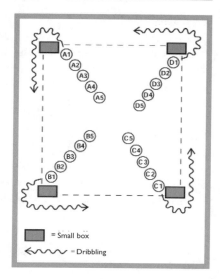

= Small box
= Dribbling

- At a sign from the coach, the first player in each group throws a dice and notes the number thrown on the sheet of paper, which is in the corner of the playing area. Each first player takes his/her ball and dribbles around the playing area. A player cannot throw a die again until he/she has dribbled the ball all the way round.
- The second player throws the dice immediately after the first, without waiting for the first to complete the circuit. The second player adds his/her throw to the first one and sets off to dribble around the playing area. The other players follow the example of the first two in sequence.
- The winning team is the one the first one to score at least 100 points, with all players and their balls back in the starting zone.

Note

- If the coach does not make clear that the throws are to be added immediately, it may happen that players (especially very young ones) simply write down their throws and do not know when they have reached 100 points.
- Younger players may have problems with the addition. At club practice sessions, parents of under-7s could possibly help by keeping score.
- In schools, players who are excused participation on grounds of health or injury could act as referees or scorers.
- Foam dice can be bought in toy shops or by mail order from dealers in sports goods. If necessary, however, small dice can also be used.

Variation I

The game is finished when the last team reaches 100 points. This means that not only the winner is clear but also the second, third and fourth positions. It is advisable to introduce a time limit, so that three teams do not have to wait for one very slow one to finish. The end of the game could be defined as one minute after the first team finishes.

Variation 2

The teams must score exactly 100. If a team has 99 points it must throw a "1" to win. If the next player throws a number larger than 1, he/she must dribble another round before throwing the dice again. This can make the finish very exciting. A team may arrive in the vicinity of 100 very quickly and be unable to throw the necessary "1."

Variation 3

The game can be played to 50 or any other number of points. This is useful if the coach wants to play several rounds. However, the target score is also dependent on the number of players. A school class with 28 players will soon reach 100, while a soccer team with 16 players will take a long time to reach 50.

Variation for advanced players
100-points dribbling with additional tasks

- The 100-points dribbling game becomes more interesting when the players have to carry out additional tasks.
- A slalom course or small obstacles could be set up in the middle of the playing zone.
- The coach should not make the task too difficult. It should simply serve to increase the dribbling time per round and make a slight additional demand on the players' technique.
- Under no circumstances should the task cause files to build up. The tasks should be easily understandable and can be demonstrated or tried out once before starting.

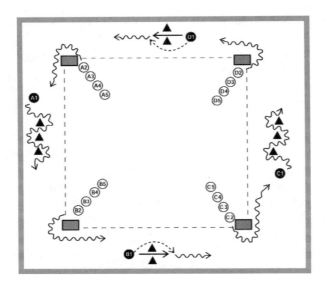

WARM-UP GAME 14: GREETINGS

This is a very different type of warming up

The players run or dribble toward teammates and greet them in a variety of playful ways. This game satisfies two requirements of specific coaching for young players. It sets the mood for the practice session in a fun way and removes any fears the players may have about physical contact. This is especially important for younger players who may be shy, and draws them naturally into the session.

Game sequence

The players move around (run, dribble) freely in a square (15 x 15 yards). At a sign from the coach they start a series of defined greetings.
• This game proceeds quickly and dynamically when no ball is used.
• If a ball is used the pace is slower but the coach has the opportunity to include soccer techniques in the game.

Between the greeting phases the players dribble freely and try out various tricks.

The players dribble:
• freely/only with the right foot/only with the left foot;
• alternately with right and left, changing after each step.

The coach takes care that the ball remains near the player during the greeting.

Examples of greetings
• Shake hands
• High fives (right hand / left hand)
• High fives with both hands
• Foot sole to foot sole (in front of/behind the body)
• Shoulder to shoulder
• Back to back
• Bow (polite waiter)

Fun greetings
• Rotate arm in arm
• Lay one hand on each other's heads
• Touch each other's ear lobes

Who wins
- The player who makes the most contacts in 30 seconds wins.
- The players who shake more than 30 hands in 1 minute win

Notes
- A musical accompaniment can be used indoors. In this case the coach can announce the next type of greeting by stopping the music and demonstrating the next movement.
- Greetings with one hand or foot should be carried out first with the right and then with the left.

WARM-UP GAME 15: SURPRISE TAG

Hunting in pairs without a ball
- Pairs of players sit or stand in a square (20 x 20 yards)
- If a hare is tagged, he/she counts out loud from 21 to 25 before he/she can chase after the tagger.
- If a hare who is being followed by a hunter stands or sits beside a pair., he/she is free. The players then swap roles.

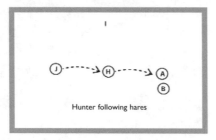

Hunter following hares

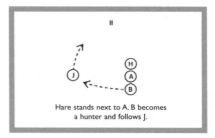

Hare stands next to A. B becomes a hunter and follows J.

- The player in the pair who is furthest away sprints toward the hunter, who now becomes a hare.
- The number of hares and hunters depends on the size of the group. No more than three hares and hunters should be in action, however, otherwise things become too confused.

Example
A hare sprints to a pair because he/she wants to escape from a hunter. The hare stands next to A. B then sprints toward the hunter, who now also changes roles and seeks to escape.

Variations (with ball)
When the players have grasped how the game works, each player is given a ball.

- In phase 1,each player carries the ball. The hunter tags a hare by touching him/her with his/her ball. The ball must not be thrown.
- In phase 2,the game becomes a dribbling game. All the balls are on the ground. A hare can only be tagged by a hunter with the ball at his/her feet.
- Another variant is to have more hunters than hares. The hunters can be recognized by the fact that they carry the ball. The hares have to dribble. A tagged hare picks his/her ball up and the hunter drops his/her ball to the ground and becomes a hare. The new hunter must hunt a hare other than the player who just tagged him/her.

WARM-UP GAME 16: DRIBBLING THROUGH THE GOAL

- The players dribble freely in pairs (player 1 and player 2).
- The coach calls, for example, "2." Players with the number 2 are then hunters.
- The players with the number 1 then dribble as fast as they can through the goals. If a player can dribble through three goals before being tagged by his/her partner, he/she scores one point.

Small Warm-Down Games

Introduction

A practice session does not always have to end with a game of 8 against 8. Small competitive games with soccer-specific elements are also suitable for rounding off the session. The players compete, have fun and use soccer techniques in a game with simple rules.

GAME 1: BURNOUT

Basic rules with a ball
- The first player of team A (the runners) kicks a ball to team B in the playing area and sets off to run through the four squares to the finish.
- Team B (field players) tries to score a goal.
- The goal should be placed at an angle to the field players so that the task of shooting into the goal is not too easy.
- When a field player scores a goal, the second runner sets off, and so on.
- Players who are between squares when a goal is scored are burnt out and have to go to the back of their team without scoring a point.
- A player who reaches the finish successfully without being burnt out scores one point. If he/she reaches the finish without stopping in one of the squares, i.e., if he/she runs from the start to the finish before a goal is scored, he/she scores 4 points. The maximum number of runners in a square at any one time cannot exceed three.

Burnout with dribbling
- When the players are familiar with the basic rules, the coach can make the game into a dribbling game by giving each runner a ball. The runners thus become dribblers.
- A dribbler must reach a square with his/her ball before a field player scores a goal. The dribblers soon learn how to run with the ball at their feet and to stop when necessary.

Burnout with tasks for the field players
The field players can also be given an additional task. Goals only count when the ball is played in a given manner before the shot at goal.

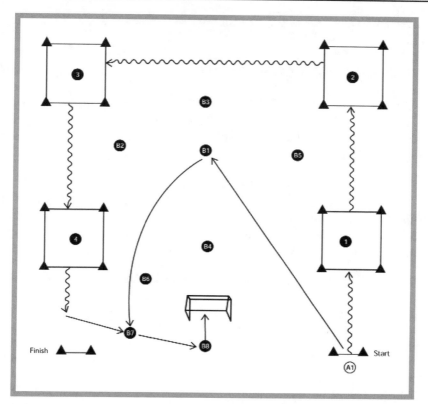

Headers

• The coach can specify how the goal has to be scored. For instance, the players might be told to pick up the ball and head it to the next player. They would also have to head it into the goal.

Passing techniques

• The ball can only be played with the inside of the foot, or the instep, or the left foot, or might have to be drop-kicked.

"Professional version" with obstacles for the runners

• To make the task of the runners or dribblers more difficult, obstacles can be placed in the runners' path. For example:
• The players have to overcome a hurdle with the ball.
• The players have to kick the ball against a small or large box before they dribble any further. (Suitable for indoors.)
• The dribblers play the ball through a small goal, run round the goal, then dribble the ball to a square.

If a task is not carried out properly, the player is burnt out. A player who misses the box or leaves out a cone on the dribbling course is also burnt out and has to join the back of the team.

GAME 2: GOALKEEPER BURNOUT

In this adaptation of "Burnout," the emphasis is on the goalkeeping techniques of throwing, catching and punching the ball, as well as throwing the ball in. After all, young players should be given as varied a soccer education as possible.

Variation 1: Throwing (small playing area - 20 x 20 yards)
- The first runner throws a ball into the playing area and runs from square to square (the squares should measure 2 x 2 yards).
- Players who reach the finish without being burnt score one point.
- A player who reaches the finish without stopping scores 4 points.

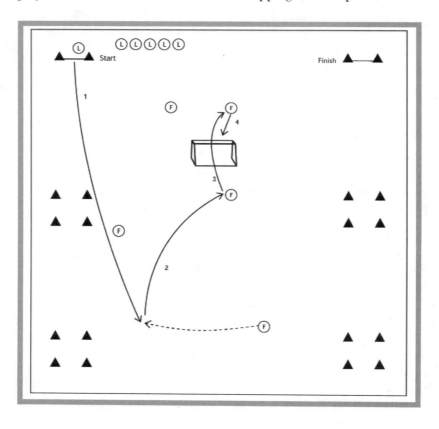

- If the ball bounces outside the playing area, the thrower is burnt out.
- Runners who are between squares when the ball enters the goal are burnt out and have to go to the back of their team. They do not drop out, therefore, but they also do not score a point.

Playing time
Each team plays for a specified time (e.g. 7 minutes).
The team with the most points wins.

Variant 2: Shooting and throwing (playing area 40 x 30 yards)

Game description
The first player of team A (the runners) drop-kicks or drop-volleys or throws a ball into the playing area. As in variant 1, he/she runs from square to square. If the ball lands in the playing area, the field players throw or shoot it into the goal as quickly as possible.

Additional rule
If the field players catch the ball, the runner is burnt out and has to go to the back of the team without scoring a point.

Variations
- Additional task for the runners: The runners are given a second ball and dribble or bounce it around the playing area.
- With goalkeeper: A runner goes in goal and tries to prevent the field players from scoring a goal. Only one shot is allowed, then the next runner starts. If the field players score they are awarded 2 bonus points.
- To make the task more difficult, the field players' goal can be placed facing away from the playing area so that the task of shooting into the goal is not too easy.

GAME 3: CATCH THE DRIBBLER

As in the "Burnout" game, a team of field players and a team of dribblers compete against each other.
- The dribblers stand on the start line (e.g. the goal line) with a ball.
- The first dribbler has a second ball, which he/she kicks far into the playing area. He/she and his/her teammates immediately dribble from the start line to a turning point and try to dribble over the finish line before the field players shoot into the goal.
- The field players are awarded one point for each dribbler who has not reached the finish when the goal is scored. The game is repeated until each dribbler has a turn at kicking the ball into the playing area, then the teams swap roles. The field players become dribblers and vive versa.
- The team that scores the most points wins.

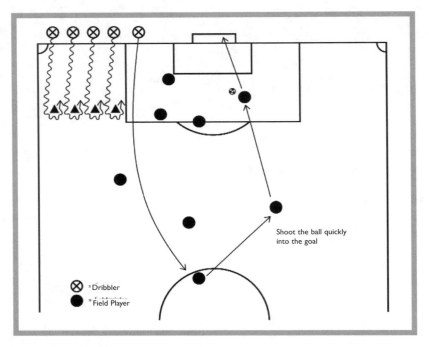

Shoot the ball quickly into the goal

⊗ = Dribbler
● = Field Player

Notes on the method
The coach should place the dribblers' turning point at a distance that gives each team a fair chance of winning. If all of the dribblers always reach the finish line, the turning point is too close to the start line. If none of the dribblers reach the finish line, the turning point is too far from the start line. In the second case the coach can shorten the distance or make the field team's task more difficult (e.g. stand the goal at an angle).

The following can be used as a goal:
Small box (indoors) on its side, either open to the playing area or closed to it; mat against the wall; two flag poles or cones; goal with net, facing into playing area or away from it, so that a direct shot into the goal is not possible and the ball has to be kicked past the goal before a goal can be scored.

GAME 4: ALASKA

"Alaska" requires the players to kick the ball with the instep, run with the ball in a small space, dribble quickly and sidefoot the ball.

Game rules
• The first dribbler receives two balls (see illustration. He/she kicks one into the playing area and dribbles the other one around his/her teammates. He/she scores a point for each completed circuit of his/her teammates.
• The ball kicked into the playing area must land in the area (the size of the area should be appropriate to the number of players). This prevents the kicker from kicking the ball so far that it cannot be reached; it then takes too long to get the game started again, and the players may become bored and frustrated. Obviously this problem does not arise indoors as the ball simple bounces back from the wall.

The field players can be given different tasks
• If a field player catches the ball, the kicker is not awarded a point. If the ball is not caught, the field player who gets to the ball first places his/her foot on it.

Fig. I: Start of Alaska

- His/her teammates stand facing him/her in a line.
- The player with the ball sidefoots it through the legs of his/her teammates. The last in the line takes the ball on with his/her foot, dribbles quickly along the line toward the kicker and calls out "Stop!"
- Meanwhile the other team's player continues dribbling round his/her group, collecting points for himself/herself and his/her team.
  When all players have had a turn, the teams swap roles. The team with the most points wins.

Variations

- The field players can be given different tasks. The first player to reach the ball might dribble around his/her teammates and finally shout "Stop." The coach must ensure that the teammates stand still. Experience has shown that young players try to shorten the dribbling stage by running around the dribbler.
- The start can be changed by getting a neutral player to throw the ball from a distance of 5 to 7 yards so that the first player can volley it into the playing area. The first player then takes the second ball and dribbles around his/her teammates.

Creative coaches of young soccer players will certainly think up other variations.

GAME 5: RUNAROUND

The rules of "Runaround" are so flexible that the game is suitable for all age
and skill levels, from beginners to experienced players. It does not need a lot
of space and can be played indoors as
well as out. Competitions and tournaments can be held outdoors. The players should first practice the basic techniques without scoring points. No goal
with a net is needed. Cones mark the
zones and the goal area.

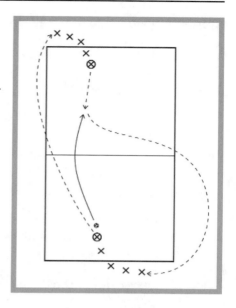

Note
The playing area can also be used for
coaching drills. For example, the coach
can ask the players to practice volley-
ing, or controlling the ball with the chest or thigh or head. This gives the
players the confidence to play the game according to the rules for advanced
or experienced players.

Game rules for beginners
The first player in zone A drop-volleys the ball (instep) over the center line.
The ball should be at least head high. He/she then runs to the other side and
joins the back of the line. The first player in zone B tries to catch the ball. If
the ball falls to the ground, a point is deducted from his/her starting total (2
to 10 points, depending on the coach's objective). The player runs to the
other side and joins the back of the line. And so on.

Who wins?
• The first player to lose all his/her points is the loser. The game then starts
again.
• The players drop out when they lose all their points. The last two players
left in are the winners.

Variations
• The ball must bounce once before it is caught.
• When the ball bounces, the player has to flick the ball up with his/her foot,
thigh or head before catching it.

Game rules for advanced players
- The basic rules are the same as for beginners.
- After the ball bounces, the player returns it to the other side without using his/her hands.
- Before returning the ball, the player can keep it in the air with as many contacts as he/she likes. However, it is advisable to return the ball as quickly as possible.

Who wins?
- The first player to lose all his/her points is the loser. The game then starts again.
- The players drop out when they lose all their points. The last two players left in are the winners. The final two players can also continue, taking turns to kick the ball and return it. Each time a player makes an error, his/her opponent is awarded a point. The first player to score two points is the winner.
- The first player to win three games is king.

Game rules for experienced players
- The basic rules are the same as for beginners and advanced players.
- The ball must not touch the ground. The players estimate where the ball will land and run to meet it. They control the ball with the foot, thigh or head and play it back into the other zone with the instep or the inside of the foot.

Variations
- Only two ball contacts are allowed (controlling touch and return).
- The ball must be returned directly (one contact only).
- The coach specifies the technique to be used to return the ball (instep or inside of foot).

Who wins?

- Each player starts with only one point, and thus drops out after only one error.
  Note: If this option is chosen, the number of players per zone should not exceed five. The coach should set up more zones, so that as many players as possible are in action.
- The players drop out when they lose all their points. The last two players left in are the winners. The final two players can also continue, taking turns to kick the ball and return it. Each time a player makes an error, his/her opponent is awarded a point. The first player to score two points is the winner.

GAME 6: SOCCER TENNIS WITHOUT A NET

Preliminary remarks

- Soccer tennis without a net is easy to understand, easy to organize and is a very effective means of improving technique.
- It can be played on a soccer pitch or on any free space as a competition between individuals or as a tournament for teams.

The player's positions

Up to 20 players (in 10 groups) can play simultaneously in one half of a soccer pitch. It is advisable to use the existing markings (goal line, side line, penalty area lines and center line).

Materials

Alongside the balls, only cones are needed, to mark out the playing areas (see illustration).

Organization

The playing area is marked with cones and measures 5 x 5 yards. Two players face each other. One of them holds a ball.

- The player holding the ball drop-volleys it toward the other player to start the game. The game is also restarted after each interruption by drop-volleying the ball.
- The ball must be played at least 18 inches above head height.
- The ball must only be allowed to bounce once.
- After it bounces, the ball must be played back with one touch. This touch can be with the foot, thigh or head.
- If the ball lands outside the playing area, the kicker's opponent scores one point. If a player makes an error, his/her opponent scores one point.

Who wins?
- The winner is the player who scores the most points in a given time.
- The winner is the first player to reach 15 points.

Variations
- After the ball bounces, the receiving player can keep it in the air by play-ing it as often as he/she wants with the foot, thigh or hand before playing it back.
- The playing area can be expanded to 10 x 10 yards. A third player is intro-duced. The ball must be volleyed by the players in a given sequence. If a player cannot volley the ball to the next player in the sequence, he/she loses one point. If a player reaches a given number of minus points, he/she drops out.

Tasks
Depending on their levels of skill and development, the players can be assigned various tasks. The coach can ask players to use the left or right foot, volley the ball with the inside of the foot, the instep or the outside of the foot, and control it with the instep, inside of the foot, outside of the foot, thigh, chest, head, etc.

Notes on the method
Two key aspects are in the forefront during the game:
- The players have fun and are thus motivated for the following phases of the practice session.
- The players can be encouraged to play this game or use elements of it in their free time to enjoy themselves. Coaches should encourage players to practice like this outside of supervised practice sessions.

The following skills can also be practiced in this game:
- accurate, carefully weighted kicking;
- ball control;

- positional play, e.g. where to stand so as to cover as large an area as possible;
- constantly changing position, depending on where the ball is;
- taking up a new position in time to get behind the ball before playing it;
- targeted exploitation of opponents' positional errors.

GAME 7: DRIBBLERS VERSUS JUGGLERS

Introduction

In this game one team (the dribblers) determines the time that the other team (the jugglers) has available to score points. A key element of this game is the pressure of time exerted by the dribblers on the jugglers by performing their dribbling tasks as quickly as possible. While the dribblers complete a tiring but technically simple task, the jugglers have to carry out a technically demanding task requiring good coordination and a lot of concentration.

Game rules

- The coach forms 2 teams with equal number of players.
- The coach gives the start signal and all players of team A dribble together around a square (length of sides: 10 - 15 yards).
- At the same time the first player of team B juggles a ball. Each ball contact with foot, thigh or head scores one point.
- The ball may touch the ground, but contact with the hands is not allowed. If the ball remains on the ground it must be played into the air with the foot.
- When the last dribbler crosses the finishing line the coach stops counting the juggler's ball contacts.
- After 2 to 4 completed dribbling circuits (depending on the size of the team), the teams swap roles so that the dribblers have a period of rest.
- Each player has a turn at juggling. If there is an odd number of players the coach selects one player to juggle twice.
- The coach records the number of ball contacts of each juggler.
- The team with the most ball contacts is the winner.

The dribblers have to dribble around the square as fast as they can, so that the jugglers have as little time as possible to accumulate points. The juggler tries to achieve as many ball contacts as possible before the stop signal is given.

Organization: Dribblers versus jugglers

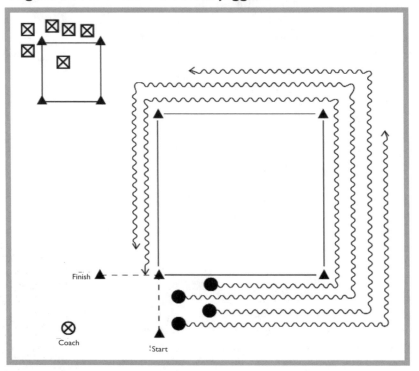

Dribbling variations
- The coach can vary the dribblers' tasks.
- The circuit around the square can be made into a slalom course with cones.

The basic principles must be retained
- All players must simultaneously carry out a task that is also physically demanding.
- The task must be relatively simple, so that the coach can concentrate on counting the number of ball contacts by the juggler.

Variation: Dribblers versus jugglers tournament

The coach organizes three equally strong teams for a tournament. The teams have to dribble, juggle and count.

Round 1: Team A dribbles, team B juggles and team C counts.
Round 2: Team B dribbles, team C juggles and team A counts.
Round 3: Team C dribbles, team A juggles and team B counts.

Each player of the counting team counts one juggler's ball contacts. As usual, the time depends on the dribblers.
The team with the most ball contacts wins.

GAME 8: BEAT THE DRIBBLERS

A) Dribbling versus direct play

As in the dribblers versus jugglers game, the follows rules apply:
• Team A carries out a task that requires coordination and technique. A point is scored for each ball contact.
• The players of team B all carry out a task that makes physical demands on them. The time available to team A depends on how quickly team B carries out its task.
• The task carried out by team B must be relatively simple, so that the coach can concentrate on counting the number of ball contacts by group A.
• The coach gives the start signal and the players of team A start to pass the ball back and forth to each other while the players of team B dribble around a square or a rectangle as quickly as possible.
• The players of team A pass the ball as quickly as possible. Each ball contact scores one point.
• The players of team B are not allowed to play the ball inside the marked square or rectangle.
• Each player has to run round a turning point before he/she can pass the ball again.

B) Dribbling versus heading

The first player of team A holds the ball in his/her hand and waits for the start signal. He/she throws the ball in the air and heads it to a teammate, then sprints to the other side. The teammate catches the ball, throws it in the air and heads it back to the starting point, and so on. Each ball contact scores one point for team A.

Direct passing through pairs of cones

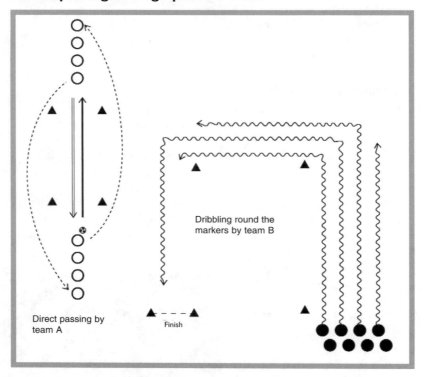

Dribbling round the markers by team B

Direct passing by team A

Finish

Variation for more advanced players

Only when a header is returned directly to the other side is a point scored. The first contact, when the ball is thrown in the air and headed, does not score a point. If the ball falls to the ground the next player restarts by throwing the ball in the air and heading it.

Examples of other tasks

• The players throw the ball back and forth with both hands.
• The players drop-volley the ball (inside of the foot or instep).
• The ball is drop-kicked back and forth.

GAME 9: FLATBALL

• The playing area is divided into 3 zones. In the middle zones are the goal-keepers, who are chosen by the coach.
• The players in the outside zones have to shoot low (below hip height) past the goalkeepers as often as possible.
• Each time a player succeeds in shooting through the middle zone to the other side, he/she scores one point.
• When a goalkeeper stops a shot, he/she changes places with the shooter.
• The player with the most points wins.

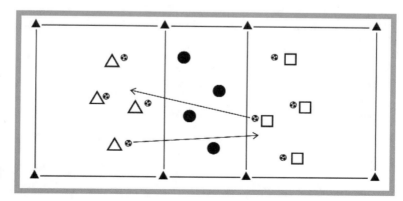

Flatball

GAME 10: FOUR-GOAL GAME

• Each team (5 - 7 players) defends 2 goals.

Note:
This game teaches the players to use all the available space and to switch the play quickly from one side to another.

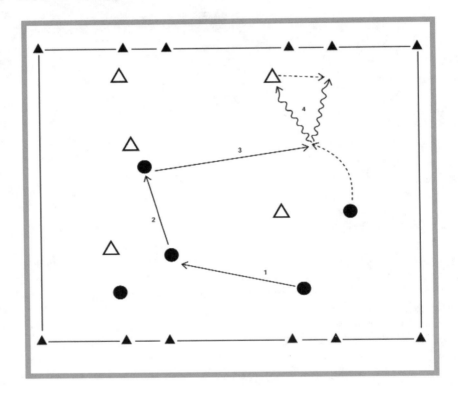

GAME 11: TARGET SHOOTING

- Two teams try to knock the balls from the cones, which are placed on the center line, by shooting at them from a distance of 5 to 10 yards.
- Shots must be taken from the shooting line.

This game improves shooting accuracy and is a lot of fun. It is important to select the right distance to shoot from. If a ball comes to rest inside the shooting distance, it should be taken back to the shooting line. No shots should be taken from a distance closer than the shooting line.

When a team has knocked more than half the balls off the cones, the next round starts. The first team, to score 3 (or 5, or 10) points is the winner.

GAME 12: HANDBALL AND HEADING WITHOUT A GOALKEEPER

- Two teams play against each other. There are 2 goals. The players throw the ball.
- The players are not allowed to bounce the ball or run more than 3 steps while holding the ball.
- Goals can only be scored with headers.
- In the goal area (marked by cones), the defenders can only play the ball by heading it.

GAME 13: THROWING TO HIT

- The players try to throw the ball over a neutral zone so that it hits an opponent.
- Each hit scores one point.
- If an opponent catches the ball, this does not count as a hit.
- A hit is only valid if the ball does not bounce before it reaches the opponent.
- The coach counts the valid hits and names the winner.

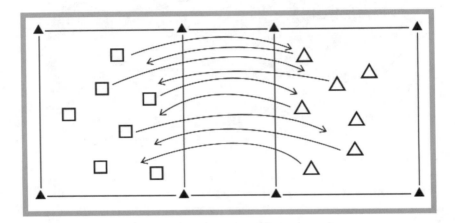

GAME 14: ONE-GOAL GAME WITH GOALKEEPER

This game combines lots of elements of street soccer. The players have lots of opportunities to react to soccer situations and gain experience in defensive and attacking play.

Organization
Each team consists of 3 to 5 players.
A neutral goalkeeper stands in the goal, which can be 5 yards wide or a normal goal. A line 25 yards from the goal line marks the limit of the playing area.

Advantages of this game
- Up to 20 players can be involved at the same time on just half of a normal pitch.
- The game is easy to understand and can be organized quickly.
- As well as balls and goals, only cones are needed (to mark the limits of the playing area). Colored overvests are also advisable for the purpose of distinguishing the teams.

- Because the playing area and the teams are small, each player has lots of ball contacts and is actively involved.
- The players can all grasp and follow defensive and attacking situations and actions.
- All players have to carry out both defensive and attacking tasks, so even the weaker players have a responsible role within their team.
- The players can use the experience gained to practice together in their free time outside of organized coaching sessions.

In this game the field players can practice the following skills:

- Taking a pass and running on with the ball under control.
- Retaining possession and combining with teammates.
- Running wide or forward to find space, and checking to the teammate who has the ball.
- Dribbling to make space for a shot.
- Taking up good defensive positions in relation to teammates, so that the total defensive area as possible is covered.
- Switching quickly between defense and attack when the ball is won or lost.
- Reacting quickly to opponents' actions.
- Making good use of scoring opportunities.

Game rules

- Before the game starts, the coach decides which team will attack first.
- After a goal is scored, a new attack is started from the attacking line.
- The goalkeeper kicks the ball randomly into play when he/she gains possession. If defenders gain possession, they can pass back to the goal-keeper or pass it toward the attacking line. If a defender intentionally kicks the ball a long distance over this line, the attackers are awarded a 7-yard (or 11-yard) penalty kick.
- Headed goals count double.

Variations

- After an agreed time the teams swap roles.
- The teams swap roles each time a goal is scored.
- The teams swap roles after three attacks fail to produce a goal.
- A player can only score a goal after taking a pass from a teammate.
- Every attacker must have at least one ball contact before a goal-scoring attempt is made.
- A neutral zone is marked in front of the goal. The field players must not enter this zone.
- Both teams attack and defend at the same time.
- No neutral goalkeeper is provided. One of the players of the defending team has to play in goal, so the defending team has one field player less

than the attackers.

Who wins?

• The team that scores the most goals wins.

GAME 15: LINE DRIBBLING

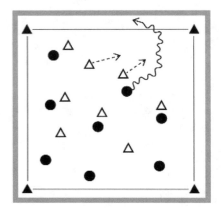

• The players are divided into 2 teams of 4 to 8 players.
• The playing area measures 20 x 40 yards.
• The goal line is between the cones marking the end of the playing area.
• A goal is scored when a player dribbles over the goal line of the opposing team.
• Shooting or passing the ball over the goal line is not allowed.

GAME 16: KINGS AND SOLDIERS

This game is very popular with younger players. Again, the aim is to hit an opponent with the ball or avoid being hit. In this case the ball is not thrown but kicked from the ground or drop-volleyed or drop-kicked. The young players learn how to react when a ball is kicked at them and how to catch a ball (this is very important for goalkeepers).

Organization

Team A plays against team B. The inner zone measures 20 x 10 meters and has a center line. Around this inner zone is the attacking zone of the opposing team. At the ends of the playing area are the kings of the two teams. A light ball or a softball is used.

Game rules

• At the start of the game, the king and his field players (soldiers) play the ball back and forth 3 times across the opposing field players. If this is achieved, the attackers try to "shoot" the opposing players.
• All players have one point.
• The ball is kicked from the ground.

- If a player is hit by the ball, he/she goes into his/her team's attacking area and helps his/her king to hit players of the other team.
- When a player catches the ball, this is does not count as a hit. The player must not drop the ball.
- When all the players of one team have been shot, the king goes into the inner zone. When the king has also been shot, the other team has won.
- If a shot hits 2 players, both have to leave the inner zone.
- If a second player catches the ball before it falls to the ground after a hit, this saves the player who was hit.
- Variation: Drop-kicks or drop-volleys are allowed.

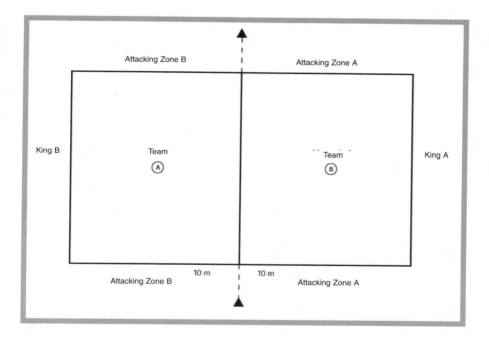

Variation: Reverse International Soccer

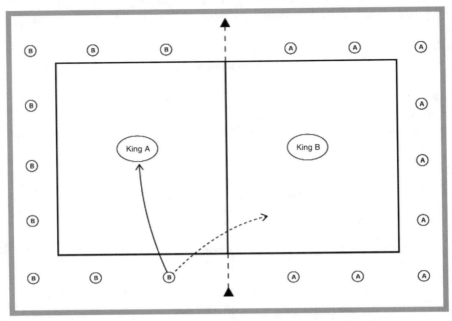

B hits the King of A and can now enter the field to help his/her king.

In this variant the king is in the inner zone and the players are in the outer zone. The aim is for all players to get into the inner zone. If a player in the outer zone shoots a player in the inner zone, the shooter enters the inner zone and the shot player is banished to the outer zone. The more players enter the inner zone, the easier it is for the players in the outer zone to shoot someone. Players are thus constantly interchanging between zones.

The game ends after an agreed time or when the last player in the outside zone hits an opponent.

Indoor Games

The prevailing circumstances in any given indoor facility will influence the organization and content of the practice sessions held there. For example, basketball courts are marked out in many sports halls. A coach can easily ensure that one or two players are meaningfully occupied at the baskets of such courts (see game I 4). When the weather is not suitable for outside practice sessions, a sports hall is ideal for coaching young soccer beginners, provided the coach makes use of the available aids and apparatus and integrates them usefully and methodically into the coaching program. Many variations that are unsuitable outdoors, where there are no suitable walls or apparatus, can be used to introduce varied and stimulating elements. All warm-up games and many small sided games can be played indoors. Some games are especially suitable for an indoor setting, because they make use of the walls, apparatus and equipment available indoors.

INDOOR GAME I: GLADIATOR

In a playing area measuring 9 by 18 yards, referred to as the gladiator field, five small boxes are arranged like dots on a dice (see diagram).

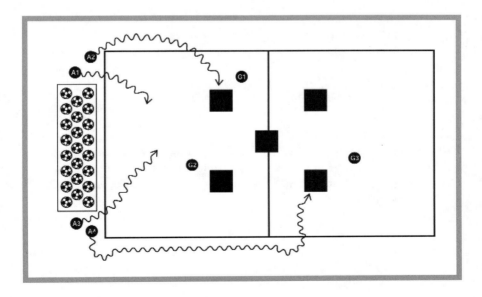

Organization
- Outside the gladiator field is a depot (e.g. the top of a box, or a trolley) with sufficient balls. Use volleyballs, basketballs, etc. if necessary).

Description of the game
- Team A (4 - 7 players) tries to take as many balls as possible past the 2 or 3 neutral players into the small boxes within an agreed time.
- Only balls that stay in the boxes are counted.
- Once a ball is in a box, it cannot be taken out again.
- Ball contacts are only allowed with the feet (dribble, then lift the ball into the box with one foot or both feet).
- More advanced players lift the ball into the box with the tip of one foot, while beginners clamp the ball between both feet and jump in the air.
- A ball in an outside box scores 1 point, and a ball in the center box scores 3 points. The gladiators should therefore guard the center box especially carefully.
- The gladiators are not allowed to leave the gladiator field. The attackers are therefore safe when they are outside the field. Inside the field, the gladiators kick away any ball they can reach.
- The attackers have to fetch the balls that are kicked away by the gladiators.
- When an attacker deposits a ball in one of the boxes, he/she fetches another one from the depot.

When the agreed time has elapsed, the next team takes its turn, etc.
The team that scores the most points wins.

Variation 1: Gladiators play against 2 teams
Two teams of 3 to 6 players start simultaneously from 2 sides and play against 2 or 3 gladiators.
Each team should use a different type of ball, e.g. differently colored or marked balls.

Variation 2: A against B
Teams A and B each nominate 2 or 3 gladiators, who defend the boxes against the 4 to 7 attackers of the opposing team. A team thus consists of 6 to 10 players, split up into attackers and gladiators. The playing time is again 2 to 5 minutes.

INDOOR GAME 2: BILLIARDS SOCCER

Depending on the size of the sports hall, two teams defend 3 to 5 goals (marked by cones, flags, etc.), which are positioned 1 or 2 yards from the wall. (The further the goals are from the wall, the harder it is to score a goal.)

Variation 1: Give-and-go using the wall

A goal is only valid if it is scored after a give-and-go using the wall instead of a second player. This scorer is under pressure of time, as he/she has to score before an opponent can reach the ball.

Variation 2: Second attacker

A goal is only valid if a second attacker beats the defenders to the ball after it bounces back off the wall and through the goal. This forces the attacker to take account of the position of the second player and chose the angle of his/her shot accordingly.

Notes

- The wall behind the goal should be even. Goals near corners are especially interesting, because the ball can bounce off 2 walls before passing through the goal. The players thus learn about angles of incidence and rebound while playing.
- The hall can optimally used by introducing as many small goals as possible.
- The use of 2 balls encourages the players to spread out and be aware of their surroundings rather than just the ball.
- Billiard soccer improves the players' ability to run into and use free space. This game is also suitable for practicing give-and-go passing at the end of a practice session.

INDOOR GAME 3: HIT THE CONES

The walls prevent the balls from rolling away very far. Balls that miss the target always come back within reach of the player.

Game rules

- Two teams stand behind a line. Each player has a ball.
- The players shoot at a line of cones, trying to knock them over. A point is awarded for each cone that is knocked over.
- The players must remain behind the shooting line.
- When all of the cones have been knocked over the game is finished.

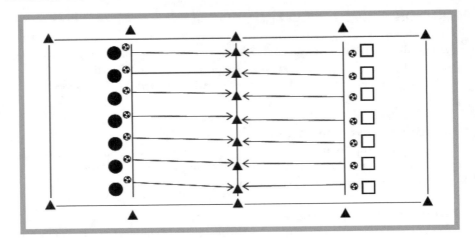

Variation

The cones are placed on benches between the two teams. Because the cones are raised, they are more difficult to hit. However, counting is easier, as the coach can see exactly how many cones are lying in each zone afterwards.

INDOOR GAME 4: HIT THE BASKET

Introduction

During an indoor soccer practice session, the coach can let all players have a turn at the basketball basket. If there are, for example, 4 baskets, a tournament could be organized for 8 players while the other players engage in another game (e.g. soccer tennis).

The following elements can be practiced in this game:
- Feel for the ball and ball control
- Kicking the ball accurately and with the right weight
- Heading
- Controlling a pass with the foot, thigh and head
- Quick reactions and constant change of position depending on the flow of play
- Getting into position before the ball arrives, so that the body is behind it.

Solo game for beginners

Player A stands about 5 yards from the basket and holds the ball in his/her hands.

Game rules

- A throws the ball up, lets it bounce and tries to play the bouncing ball with his/her foot and steer it into the basket.
- If A hits the backboard he/she scores one point. If he/she hits the ring of the basket he/she scores 2 points. If the ball goes into the basket he/she scores 3 points.
- A collects the rebound ball, throws it in the air and tries again, and so on.

Who wins?

- The player who scores the most points in an agreed time is the winner.
- The player who scores 15 points with the fewest attempts is the winner.

Variations

- A scores a point for catching the ball when it rebounds from the back board.
- If A controls the rebound with his/her foot, thigh, etc. he/she scores 2 points.
- A heads the ball into the basket.

Solo game for advanced players

- A tries to play the rebound ball into the basket.
- The ball can bounce a few times between attempts.
- The ball can be played with the foot, thigh and head.
- The ball can only be played with the right or the left foot.

Who wins?

- The player who scores the most points with an agreed number of attempts is the winner.
- The player who reaches 15 points with the least number of attempts is the winner.
- The player who scores most points in an agreed time is the winner.
- The player who scores 15 points fastest is the winner.

Variations

- The rebound ball can only touch the ground once, but can then be kept in the air with one contact or more with the foot, thigh or head before it is directed at the basket again.
- Before each attempt the ball can only touch the floor once. It must then be played directly at the basket.
- A point is deducted if the ball does not touch the basket ring or enter the basket.

Doubles game (suitable for more advanced players)

Organization
- Two players stand in front of the basket. Player A holds the ball.

Game rules
- The game is started or restarted by throwing the ball up and allowing it to bounce once before then trying the kick it into the basket.
- The players take turns in trying to play the ball into the basket.
- When the ball rebounds it can be allowed to bounce once or more times before another attempt is made to play it into the basket with the foot, thigh or head.
- As soon as a player sends the ball toward then basket, he/she must move aside to make room for the other player.
- The players take turns in restarting the game after a basket is scored or the game is interrupted.
- Two points are awarded for a direct basket and one for an indirect basket (ball touches the ring or the backboard before entering the basket.

Who wins?
- The player who scores the most points in an agreed time is the winner.

INDOOR GAME 5: INDOOR FLATBALL

This game can be used to practice sidefooting the ball accurately and firmly. The players should play the ball close to the benches before shooting at goal.
- The playing area is divided up by small boxes on which benches are placed.
- The end walls are the goals.

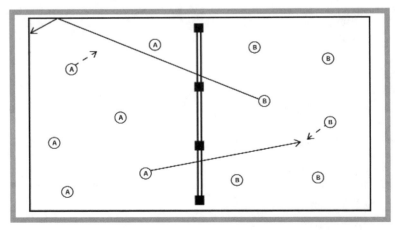

- The players try to sidefoot the ball under the benches so that it hits the wall.
- The opposing players try to stop the ball from hitting the wall. They are not allowed to use their hands.
- It is advisable to use 2 or 3 balls so that more players are always actively involved.

INDOOR GAME 6: ZONE SOCCER

The aim of this game is to involve as many young players as possible and to use the available space to full advantage. Up to 24 players can take part.

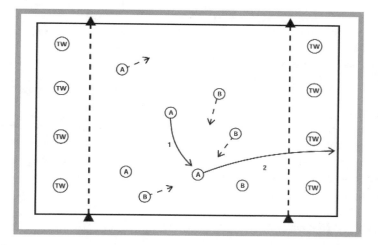

Organization

- Each team (8 to 12 players) has the same number of goalkeepers and field players.
- The goal zones are marked by cones. (Any convenient lines already present in the sports hall can be used a shooting lines.)
- The players of the goalkeeper group are between the shooting line and the goal line.
- The field players (A and B) are in the area between the shooting lines.

Game rules

- The goal is the entire wall as far up as the goalkeeper can reach. Any exist-ing markings on the wall (foam insulation, paneling) can be used to indi-cate the height of the goal. In cases of doubt the referee decides whether a goal is valid.

- Each player in the goalkeeper team can block the ball with his/her hands but cannot enter the playing area.
- The field players may not enter the goal area.
- Goals are only valid if the shot is taken in front of the shooting line in the playing area.
- The ball is out of play when it hits the wall above the height of the goal and rebounds into the playing area. The same applies when it rebounds after a goal is scored. In each case the game is restarted by a player of the goalkeeper team (throw or pass).
- An opponent may not try to intercept the restart ball.
- The field players and goalkeepers swap tasks after an agreed time (5 - 8 minutes).

Who wins?
- The group that scores the most goals in the agreed time wins.
- The team that has the best result after 1 (or 4) games wins.
- If the coach wants to focus on the goalkeepers, points can be awarded for saves. The goalkeeper that makes the most saves is then the winner.

Variations
- A second ball is introduced to increase the number of actions. The referee should try to keep both balls in view. A team's cries of joy when they score will attract the referee's attention, so that he/she will not miss a valid goal.
- The goalkeepers of one team play against the field players of the other team. This results in four games.

Advantages of zone soccer
- Lots of players can take part.
- The alternation of physical exertion (field players) and active recuperation (goalkeepers) is good for the players' conditioning. Since the goalkeepers do not have to run around, they can concentrate better on the play. The field players face a bigger technical challenge. They have to act quickly, sprint, dribble and create shooting chances in a restricted space.
- The width of the goal spreads the play and encourages lots of goalscoring attempts and incidents. As a result the players experience a lot of success moments. The goalkeepers can make lots of saves and the attackers can still score lots of goals.

Warm-up drills

Coaches at all levels frequently bemoan their players' lack of creativity and their inability to do the unexpected. They then go on to claim that lack of ability is the reason and that nothing can be done about this. "Either you have it or you don't! Creativity cannot be learned." This is not true, however.

Wide range of movements as a basis for creativity

The ability to act creatively must be cultivated by systematic and varied coaching in basic skills. Only players who have learned a variety of alternative solutions to a game situation will be able to surprise an opponent. Acquired techniques have to be practiced until they become second nature. Only then can players take their eye off the ball and act as the situation requires. The more alternative movements a player has mastered, the more creative he/she can be.

Repeated practice

In the warming-up phase of practice sessions, the players repeatedly practice basic techniques until they can use them automatically. This gives them the skill and confidence to be able to control and run with the ball and to pass, dribble and shoot accurately and quickly under pressure from opponents. During each practice session the players should carry out a selected drill for 5 to 10 minutes. The following drills are especially suitable for this purpose:
• Zigzag/comb in large groups
• Ball control in small groups and pairs
• Drills for controlling and running with the ball and improving passing techniques
• Combination drills with defined passing and running movements
Basically a coach can repeat all the techniques that the players have acquired. The players develop a feel for the ball when they regularly carry out changes of direction and turns while running with the ball. This gives them the confidence to outsmart an opponent and encourages a creative attacking attitude. The players see more, because they do not have to focus their attention on the ball all the time.

DRILL 1: ZIGZAG

The zigzag for 4 players is an interesting warm-up drill (see diagram). The dribblers meet at various points and are thus forced to take their eyes off the ball and observe the other players. It is important that the players dribble with both the left and the right foot.

The players change direction and perform turns at the cones, using the following techniques:
- Change of direction with inside of foot
- Change of direction with outside of foot
- Dummy step, step-over, scissor
- 270-degree turn with the inside of the foot
- 270-degree turn with the outside of the foot
- Drag-back with the sole of the foot
- Dragging the ball behind the standing leg
- Combination of various techniques

DRILL 2: COMB

The emphasis here is on moving forward and backward. As many 180-degree turns as possible are incorporated in a flowing continuous sequence. The coach should always repeat the dribbling directions for the first few practice runs (forward - to the middle - back - and so on).

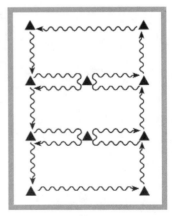

At the end of the first series the players dribble over to the other side and start their way back with the same dribbling directions.

A selection of possible technique combinations in the comb:
- 90 degrees (first and third cones)
  Change of direction with the inside of the foot / change of direction with the outside of the foot / 270-degree turn with the inside of the foot / 270-

degree turn with the outside of the foot / dummy step, step-over, scissor / drag/back with sole of foot + inside of foot
- 180 degrees (center)
Drag-back with sole of foot / change of direction with the inside of the foot / change of direction with the outside of the foot / scissor (inside - inside) / drag behind standing leg

DRILL 3: STAR

Four to six players dribble toward the center point, turn through 180 degrees one yard before the center and dribble back to their cone.

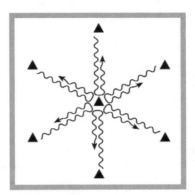

Possible techniques
- Drag back with the sole of the foot
- Change of direction with the inside of the foot
- Change of direction with the outside of the foot
- Scissor (inside - inside)
- Drag behind the standing leg

DRILL 4: DRILL FOR 2 PLAYERS - OPPONENT FROM THE SIDE

Two players practice shielding the ball. In doing so they repeat the various techniques for turning through 180 degrees (see drill 2).

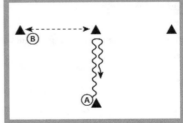

DRILL 5: OPPONENT BEHIND

In this drill the players practice changing direction with the ball while under pressure from an opponent behind them. The player with the ball dribbles between 2 comes while shielding the ball from the opponent. If players practice this regularly, they will not be nervous in similar situation in real games.

DRILL 6: DIRECTIONAL DRIBBLING

The foot and leg movements needed for dribbling the ball with an opponent behind can be practiced in series in the directional dribbling drill. After each feint (e.g. dummy step (outside - outside)) the players stop the ball briefly before repeating the same basic movement faster in the same direction. It is important that the basic movements are carried out with conviction. The coach can select the distance between the turning points as he/she wishes. A distance of 6 to 12 yards is recommended.

When the series of basic movements in one direction is finished, the players should return to the starting cone in the same sequence. They start with a feint, taking a step in one direction with the leading foot then dribbling the ball in the opposite direction with the other foot. They then stop briefly and start the next movement. By dribbling to the right and left the players improve their ability to dribble with both feet. Directional dribbling is excellent for practicing the following basic movements:
• Dummy step
• Step-over
• Scissor

Variation: Directional dribbling with a partner
All the techniques practiced in directional dribbling can be carried out with a partner. This gives the players a better feel for the game situation. The partner mimics all the movements in parallel, so the dribbler can feel the

effect of his/her feints. After 2 lengths the players swap tasks. After practicing the techniques they have learned until they are second nature, the players can try them out in small sided games until they are able to use them creatively without difficulty in a real game.

DRILL 7: ONE-TOUCH PASSING IN A SQUARE

Preliminary remarks

Fast passing sequences, if possible involving one-touch passing, improve team play within a group and improve the players' passing technique. The players engage in a series of give-and-go passes, varied with direct passes to the opposite side.

The passing sequence for one round is: Give-and-go - one-touch pass - give-and-go - one-touch pass.

A passes to M2

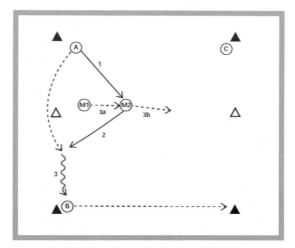

The flank players A, B and C and the wall players M1 and M2 take up their positions as shown in the diagram.
(1) A plays a give-and-go with M2.
(2) At the same time B runs to the next cone.
(3) A passes to B.
(3a) The wall player M2 runs to the cone in the center to serve as an opponent on the other side.
(3b) M1 takes up position for a give-and-go.

Direct pass to the other side

To make this a continuous drill, the sequence is continued on the other side.
(4) A passes to B on the other side.
(5) B passes to M1, who serves as a wall player. M2 challenges.
(6) B runs round M2 to take a pass from wall player M1.
(7) B dribbles to the next cone.
B passes to C on the other side and the sequence starts again. The center players sprint to a new position.

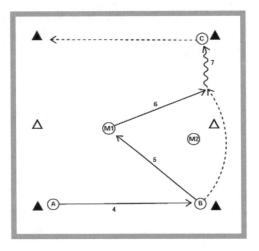

Notes on the method

- Place the cones to mark a square with sides 10 yards long.
- Place a cone in the middle of each of 2 opposite sides as an orientation point for the wall players.
- The players take up positions as shown in diagram 1.
- Explain the run paths and pass sequences step by step. The players should stop the ball after each pass before the drill starts properly.
- When the run paths and pass sequences are known, the players should always play the ball with one touch if they are confident enough to do so.
- In the final stage, the players should always play the ball with just one touch. When a player takes the return pass from the wall player, he/she plays a one-touch pass to the next player on the opposite side, who initiates a give-and-go with his/her first touch.
- The two center players should swap with 2 passers after a while, so that all players can perform all roles (passer, wall player and opponent).
- When the players have mastered the drill in one direction they should carry it out in the opposite direction.

Young players enjoy the fast sequence of one-touch passes and give-and-go passes. The tasks change quickly, all players are in motion and all players have to concentrate. For the coach this drill offers a clearly visible learning area in which he/she can observe and work to improve the level of ability of his/her players (passing accuracy, ability to play a give-and-go, stamina).

B passes to C; M1 and M2 sprint back

Coordination conditioning

Principles

Coordination drills in each practice session

In the long-term, coaches should take account of players' deficits and work systematically and regularly to eliminate them. The world of young players has changed enormously in recent decades, so coordination conditioning should be part of every practice session. Lack of exercise in general and lack of experience of activities such as climbing, rolling, hopping, skipping and balancing have resulted in a considerable coordination deficit in young players. Coaches should aim to compensate for this by the use of coordination drills, as coordination is essential to achieving top performance.

Coordination - the basis of success

A large number of muscles are needed if the body is to carry out the appropriate sports movements quickly and powerfully over a period of time. Soccer players' muscles should therefore be controlled by a well developed nervous system. Soccer players should be able to learn new soccer techniques quickly, to control them economically and precisely, and to adapt them to unpredictable events. Players with good coordination can master sports movements in a short time, under pressure time and in limited space.

Coordination conditioning (general and specific)

While general coordination conditioning involves exercises that are of importance for all sportsmen and sportswomen, coordination conditioning for soccer players should take account of the demands made by the game of soccer. In particular, the use of soccer techniques under difficult circumstances should be promoted and the players should be put under pressure (time, opponents, space, situation, complexity, physical effort).

Consequences for coaching soccer players

Coordination of movements makes demands on perception, imagination (thinking ahead, anticipating changes) and concentration. As players grow older and their skills improve, typical soccer-related demands should increasingly be placed at the heart of coordination conditioning. This means that the focus should be on soccer-specific movements (techniques) under variable conditions. The players should apply the techniques they have learned in combination with additional tasks. The coach can require them to lengthen or shorten their stride patterns and frequencies with the help of rods or tires before or after using soccer techniques and under pressure of time.

Quality of soccer-typical movements

During coordination conditioning, players should improve the quality of their soccer-typical movements.

Coordination

The typical demands imposed on soccer players by the game of soccer should be at the heart of coordination conditioning. After carrying out varied basic conditioning with general coordination exercises, the players should finish off with effective coordination conditioning with soccer-specific movements (techniques) under difficult conditions. This means that the players should use the techniques they have learned in combination with additional tasks, under additional pressures or in different circumstances. The practice sessions described in this book therefore include a phase in which regular coordination conditioning is carried out. It should be clear that coordination is the key to successful actions in sport and should therefore be given a high priority during practice sessions.

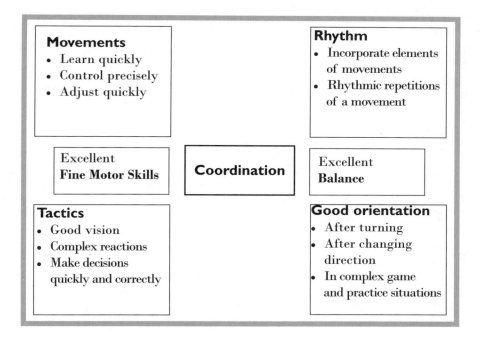

Coordination drills

GENERAL COORDINATION CONDITIONING

- Running coordination
- Coordination of arms and legs
- Varied types of movement (turning, hopping)

Drills with rods

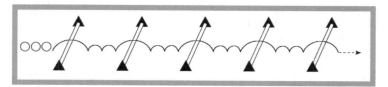

Tasks
- Run over the rods - right foot first - 3 steps in the middle
- Run over the rods - left foot first - 3 steps in the middle
- After the rods, sprint for 10 yards

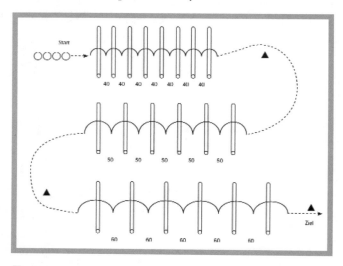

Tasks
- Run over rods placed at different intervals
- Fast turn around the cone

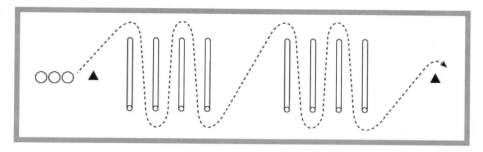

Tasks
- Run (holding the ball) in a slalom through the rods
- Dribble around the rods

Tasks
- Sprint over the rods (holding the ball)
- Drop the ball on the ground and shoot at the goal

Drills with hoops

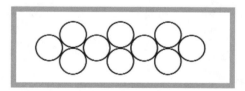

Jumping Jacks in hoop course
- Open and close legs

Arm Movements:
- Lift arms - drop arms
- Left arm forward - right arm forward

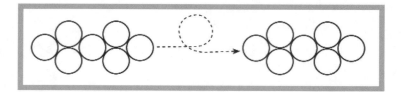

- Jumping jack with turn in the middle
- Fast orientation

COORDINATION AND WARMING UP

Easy coordination tasks should be included in the warming-up phase for young players. Drills to improve running coordination are very popular with young players, as are small dribbling games (for fun) and drills aimed at improving ball technique and orientation.

Warming up with apparatus
The coach sets up rods, hurdles, tires and cones in a square. The players dribble freely in the square.

Tasks involving hurdles
- Play the ball forward and jump over the hurdle.
- Jump over the hurdle with the ball clamped between both feet.
- Carry out a forward roll over the hurdle with the ball clamped between both feet.

Tasks involving cones
- Various feints

Tasks involving the hoop course
- Play the ball forward to the side of the course and run through the course carrying out specified movements (e.g. jumping jack)

The players dribble with various balls (soccer ball, softball, rubber ball, water ball, tennis ball) and carry out various tasks
- Dribble slowly and quickly
- Dribble in small circles using the inside and outside of the foot (clockwise and counterclockwise)
- Stop when the coach signals
- Push the ball 5 yards away and collect it
- Carry out tricks (step-over, scissor, drag-back with sole of foot)

Zipper
The zipper consists of 2 elements. On the long sides the players carry out tasks with and without a ball, while on the diagonals the two groups of players thread through each other (zipper sequence). The players adapt their speed to that of the group and maintain the correct distance from the player in front. The first player in the group has a special role, as he/she maintains the given speed and keeps his/her eyes on the first player of the other group. Both leading players ensure that the groups arrive in the middle at the same time and thread through each other. Carrying out turns while doing this helps the players to learn how to orient themselves quickly and maintain the correct distances from their fellow players. Two-player drills in the middle lead to contact and transfer phases.

Tasks in the zipper (on the diagonals)
Drills with the ball
- Carry the ball to the middle and then transfer it (group A with ball, group B without ball)
- Dribbling, each player has a ball (simple zipper sequence with dribbling).
- Dribbling, making a turn before threading through the other group.
- Transfer the ball with the foot (group A with ball, group B takes the ball over in the middle)
- Double transfer (group A dribbling, group B carrying the ball). In the middle the two groups exchange balls and the group A players continue with the ball in their hands and the group B players continue with the ball at their feet.

Individual drills with the ball
The coach specifies the type of movement (run forward/backward, hop, side-step, run lifting the knees, skip). Additional tasks, which have to be carried out before the groups meet in the middle, increase the level of difficulty.

These could be, for example, turns or jumps. A fast turn just before the groups meet conditions the players' orientation. The players have to resume their proper distance from the player in front after the turn. The players run backward through the zipper sequence, paying attention to the direction in which they are running and maintaining the correct distance to the next player, then 2 yards before the middle they turn through 180 degrees and run forward through the zipper sequence in the middle of the square.

Drills for 2 players

Players can carry out drills in pairs in the middle of the square. Contact tasks (high fives with one or both hands, frontal contact jumps, etc.), transferring the ball with hands or feet and combinations of both are just a few examples. These drills promote the players' sense of orientation and timing. The players run two by two to the middle and give each other high fives with one or both hands. They then run to the next cone. Soccer players must be able to land securely and quickly resume their running rhythm after jumping into the air. Young players derive a lot of fun from this simultaneous jumping, contact in the air and a secure landing, followed by a run, and they also condition their coordination skills.

Drills with the ball

When the players dribble through the zipper sequence they maintain their distance from the player in front. To do this they have to look up from the ball and adjust their speed to the player in front and their counterpart in the other group. A player takes the ball with both hands from the counterpart in the other group and at the same time gives him/her the second ball on the ground. This task requires good concentration if the players are to run smoothly through the middle without stumbling.

Tasks on the long sides
Without a ball
- Hopping
- Sidesteps
- Running with high knee lift
- Skipping

With a ball
- Throw the ball into the air while running
- Bounce the ball (with right hand, left hand, alternate right and left)
- Dribble (right foot, left foot, alternate right and left - one ball contact for each step)
- Dribble sideways (push the ball forward with the inside of the foot)
- Scissor, dummy step with 2 intermediate steps

RUNNING COORDINATION

Modern soccer is very fast. To be successful, players have to act quickly when they are in possession of the ball and also have to make numerous sudden changes of direction, sprints into free space and rapid switches from defense to attack. The demands are so great that special and systematic conditioning of running coordination, and especially running technique and rhythm, are absolutely necessary.

Special aspects of running coordination for soccer players

The running required of a soccer player differs considerably from that of an athlete. Jumps, turns, changes of direction, runs with the ball and tackles before or after a sprint require players to adjust their stride length and frequency to the changing game situation. This makes variable, flexible and purposeful use of running techniques necessary during a game. The soccer-specific conditioning of running coordination is thus of major importance in the coaching of young soccer players and indeed of players at all levels.

Running and jumping in a triangle of rods

Fast footwork

Targeted coaching of running coordination for soccer players must be one of the focal points during practice sessions.

Fast footwork, i.e. the fast coordination of nerves and foot muscles, is in the forefront in this drill. Small, fast steps ensure that the player is always able to choose his/her direction of running. This enables him/her to control his/her body and accelerate quickly in any direction. Good footwork is also an important prerequisite for a good shooting technique, as constant adjustment of a player's distance from the ball brings the player into the best shooting position. The players should be able to switch from a duel involving short steps to a long-striding sprint.

Triangle of hoops and rods

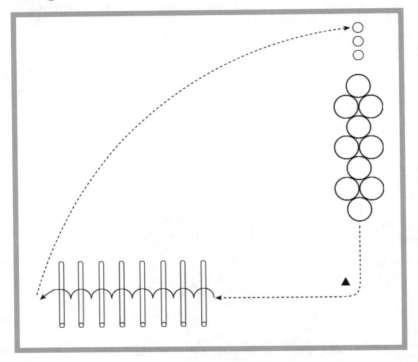

Movement tasks in the hoop course
- Jumping jack
- Two-footed jumps

Movement tasks in rod course
- Running (forward, sideward, backward)
- One-footed and 2-footed jumps
- Slalom run

SOCCER-SPECIFIC COORDINATION CONDITIONING

Drills followed by an action

After completing the course of rods and tires the player takes a pass shortly after the last jump. The player pushes a return pass, receives another pass and dribbles with the ball to the cone. The passer at the cone now runs to the start of the course.

Task A: Pass game

Task B: Give-and-go

In this variant the player takes a return pass, plays a give-and-go with the passer and dribbles to the cone at the side so that he/she can make the next pass.

Task C: Header or shot at goal

In variation C the player in the goal throws a ball to the player who sprints over the finishing line of the course. The player heads the ball so that the thrower can catch it and then swaps places with the thrower. Another variation is for the goalkeeper to throw the ball and the player to make a diving header at the goal.

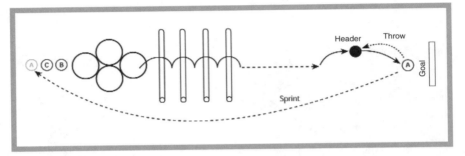

Notes on the method

The coach must continuously switch the players' tasks in the rod and tire course, so that the players repeatedly have to adjust to new conditions.

Drills with an action in the middle

In special coordination conditioning for soccer players, the players should use soccer techniques between the rod and tire courses. They perform running and jumping movements in the course and use the specified soccer technique in the middle (in this case a header to the side). This has the advantage that the players use a technique (passing, taking a pass, shooting or heading) under more difficult conditions, as their attention is diverted by the coordination movements.

Weighted passing

In this drill the players push the ball along the side of the course at a speed that allows them to cover the course and then catch the ball and carry out one or two dribbling movements. This helps them to develop a feeling for a weighted pass into the goal area - neither too fast nor too slow.

THE COORDINATION LADDER

Effective and systematic coordination conditioning for soccer players requires aids such as balls, rods, tires, hurdles and, last but not least, the coordination ladder. The coordination ladder can be set up quickly and used in a variety of ways.

Drills without a ball

Fast steps along the conditioning ladder

- Forward (one contact)/forward (two contacts)
- Run through each second or third field (variation of stride length)
- Running movements such as kicking up the heels, lifting the knees, etc.
- Running sideways (two contacts)
- Cross steps
- Backward (one contact)/backward (two contacts)

Dummy steps
- With tap (outside foot to ground)
- Without tap (stop outside foot before ground contact and pull back)

Cross Steps

Backward and forward steps with back foot
- The leading foot is placed in the fields of the coordination ladder.

- The trailing foot is moved back and forth.
- Rhythm: right foot forward - left foot backward - right foot forward - left foot forward - right foot into next field - left foot forward - and so on.

Additional tasks for the arms

As the players run along the coordination ladder they can carry out additional tasks with their arms. This increases the difficulty of the movement task. The arms are held in an unaccustomed position (to the side, upward, on the back) or moved (forward - backward, up - down, to the knee, chest, hips and back).

Jumping jack and hopping

Familiar movements are more difficult in the coordination ladder, as the players have to align their leg movements to the distances within the coordination ladder. This applies to the jumping jack as well as hopping movements.
Variation 1:
Jump in every second field of the coordination ladder.
Variation 2:
Jump in every field of the coordination ladder.
Variation 3:
Reverse jumping jack (arms open, legs together).
Variation 4:
Arms stretched alternately upward and downward in front of body.

Drills with the ball

Movement sequences with a ball are a meaningful addition to the drills with arm movements.

- The ball can be held behind the body, up or down, or against the foot or knee.
- The players can also move the ball easily (up and down or left and right). This makes the task harder and promotes the coordination of arms and legs.

Ball against inside of foot / ball against knee

Variations

While the players are running along the coordination ladder the ball can be:

- circled around the body;
- thrown up in the air;
- bounced.

The fluid running rhythm should not be interrupted by the throwing or bouncing movements.

Drills with ball and two players

The coach or another player has a ball in his/her hand and throws it (high) or pushes it (low) to the player who is running along the coordination ladder and carrying out specified movements (e.g. fast foot movements with dummy steps).

Movements in the direction of the coach
Possible soccer techniques
- Header
- Return pass with the inside of the foot (low or high)
- Return pass with instep (high)
- Hip-high volley

Coach to the side
- Header after sequence of steps or jumps along the coordination ladder
- Passes after sequence of steps or jumps along the coordination ladder
- Pass to coach - pass forward parallel to ladder - run along the coordination ladder - run onto the forward pass - dribble back

Ladder at right angle

The coordination ladder can be arranged in a right angle. This means that forward and sideward movements can be combined, e.g. dummy steps - sideward run with 2 contacts.

Drills with final action

The drills with the coordination ladder can be combined with a final technique task. The first player in the group starts on one side of the coordination ladder and the coach or another player stands at the end of the ladder with a ball. The ball should be played or thrown to the player just after he/she completes the coordination ladder run.

Variation 1: Permanent player with ball at end of ladder.

Variation 2: The runner and the player at the end of the ladder swap roles after a pass sequence or a header at the end of the ladder run.

Coordination ladder and shot at goal

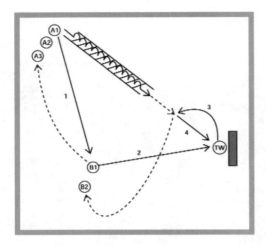

(1) A1 plays to B1 and runs along the coordination ladder.
(2) B1 plays the ball directly to the goalkeeper, who picks it up.
(3) The goalkeeper throws (or passes) the ball to A1.
(4) A1 finishes with a header, diving header or shot and takes up position
    behind B2. B1 takes up position behind A3.
A2 passes to B2.
And so on.

Complete practice sessions

Series 1: Feel for the ball - dribbling

The practice sessions in the first series are designed to impart a feel for the ball and to teach ball control, dribbling techniques, changes of direction, turns and feints. In this way the players can build up an extensive repertoire of movements. Feel for the ball helps players to learn more soccer techniques. Focusing on the ball has a positive effect on the ability to control a pass with one touch, strike the ball with just the right amount of force, shoot accurately and dribble. The players see more and develop a better tactical sense, because they are able to concentrate on more than just the ball. Drills in this series are especially suitable for warming up. It is important that the coach puts together an interesting and varied selection of organizational setups (zigzag, comb, small sided games) and techniques.

In this series the players learn:
- to run with the ball, keeping it under control and close to their feet. This can help them to grasp more of what is happening around them, so that they can pass to a teammate or give a teammate the opportunity to run into space. The players should be able to take their eyes from the ball and assess the game situation around them.
- to run as fast as possible with the ball when no opponent is near. The ball need not be close to the feet, but should always be under control. If the situation requires it, the player should be able to change direction or speed or to stop the run.

- to outsmart an opponent with a feint. This often involves a change of speed or direction together with a body movement such as dropping one shoulder.

PRACTICE SESSION B 1
BASIC DRILLS - FEEL FOR THE BALL

A) Setting the mood
Shadow dribbling (game G5) is very suitable for this practice session. The players learn to take their eyes off the ball and follow the other player (alternatives: games G1, G2)

B) Warm-up drill
As this is the first practice session in the series, the coach starts with a zigzag and explains the run paths.

Zigzag for a group of 4
The players dribble from the starting cones S1 and S2 along the zigzag course to the turning cones W1 and W2 and back again. The players can use any dribbling techniques they like. At this stage the main priority is dribbling the ball in a controlled manner round the zigzag course.

C) Coordination conditioning

The coach changes to the rod and tire course and organizes general coordination drills such as running over the rods and tires (see pp. 90 - 92).

D) Main phase: Ball control and change of direction

The coach takes the players back to the zigzag (see warm-up drill) to work at improving their technique.

Tasks

- Dribble round the course (1 round slow, 1 round fast)
- Two rounds with change of direction using inside of foot
- Two rounds with change of direction using outside of foot
- Two rounds with change of direction using inside and outside of foot alternately

Other techniques can be gradually introduced and repeatedly practiced

Zigzag in groups of 2

Here the players learn to carry out the dummy step.

(1) Two players stand at a cone. A has the ball and dribbles toward the first cone.

(2) He/she dribbles round the short zigzag course, changing direction using the inside and outside of the foot.

(3) After passing to B he/she waits at the start cone until B completes his/her round. The players change the turning direction after every 3 rounds. The coach now explains the dummy step. All the players try out this new technique and practice it intensively.

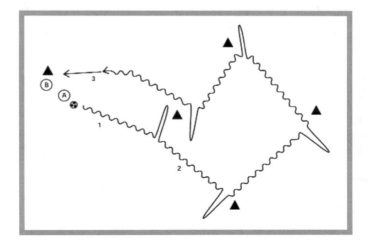

Zigzag with shot at goal

The coach sets up a zigzag course between 2 goals. At both sides, players start a run round the course and finish with at a shot at goal. The goalkeeper rolls the ball back into the path of the player, who joins the back of the next group. The more players who are involved, the longer the course should be. A second or third course can be set up so that the players can score as many goals as possible. If there are not enough goals available, goals can be marked with cones. Each player should take a turn at playing in goal. Dribbling techniques: Change of direction with the inside of the foot / outside of the foot), dummy step.

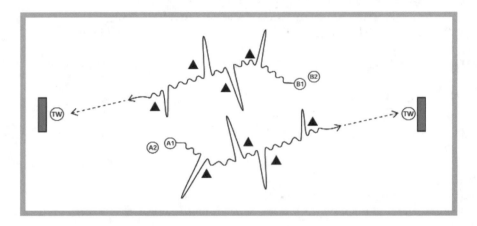

E) End game

• A 4 against 4 tournament provides plenty of opportunities for dribbling.

PRACTICE SESSION B 2:
DRIBBLING DRILLS FOR GROUPS OF 3

A) Setting the mood
Warm-up game G3: Grand prix (under-11s)
Warm-up game G2: Plague in Venice (under 15s)

B) Warm-up drill - Dribbling in zigzag in groups of 4
The players repeat the techniques they have learned in the zigzag course
(change of direction with inside of foot, change of direction with outside of
foot, dummy step) and try out tricks of their own.

C) Coordination conditioning
The coach sets the players general coordination conditioning tasks using the
rod and hoop course.

D) Main phase: Dribbling drills in groups of 3

New technique in the zigzag course - change of direction through 270
degrees with the inside of the foot
This technique involves changing direction 2 or 3 times in succession, playing
the ball with the inside of the foot. It should be carried out slowly at first,
building up speed as the players practice it more. This movement shields the
ball from an opponent (represented by a cone) until the player sets off in the
new direction toward the next cone.

Zigzag in group of 3
B dribbles in a short zigzag course and plays the ball to the outside player C.
C plays the ball back (one touch). B controls the ball and dribbles back to
the start, where he/she plays a give-and-go with A. After an agreed time (e.g.
1 minute) has elapsed, the players swap positions. The outside player carries

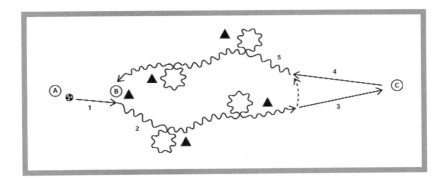

Techniques: Change of direction with the inside of the foot / outside of the foot, dummy step and turn through 270 degrees

(1) A passes to B
(2) B dribbles round the zigzag course
(3) B passes to C
(4) C passes the ball back to B
(5) B dribbles round the zigzag course

Drills in groups of 3

In this drill the players change roles after a dribble and a passing sequence with the outside player.

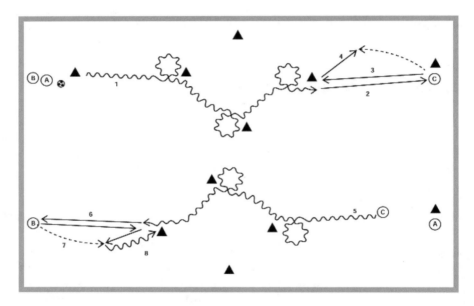

(1) Dribble round the course
(2) Pass to C
(3) C passes back to A
(4) A passes into the path of C
(5) C controls the ball and dribbles round the course.

Triangle with center

Three players dribble simultaneously toward a center point. One yard from the center they all turn left and dribble to the next cone. When they reach the cone they dribble toward the center again. After one round they repeat the sequence, turning right instead of left.

Before the players reach the center they perform a feint:
- Dummy step
- Step-over
- Turn through 270 degrees with the inside of the foot

If the number of players does not divide equally by 3 the coach can form one or 2 groups of 4 (square with center).

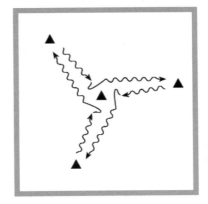

End game
The session ends with a small warm-down game (see p. 43 ff.)

PRACTICE SESSION D 3
TURNING THROUGH 180 DEGREES WITH THE BALL

A) Setting the mood
Warm-up game G5 - Shadow dribbling and/or G14 - Greetings

B) Warm-up drill - dribbling in a zigzag in groups of 4
The coach calls out the techniques that the players have to use (change of direction with the inside of the foot, change of direction with the outside of the foot, turn through 270 degrees with the inside of the foot) in a random sequence. The players have to react immediately and switch to the new technique. This drill enables the coach to assess whether the players know the terms and can switch quickly from one movement to another.

C) Coordination conditioning
The players carry out general coordination drills. (Conditioning aids: Rods, hoops, coordination ladder.)

D) Main phase: Turning through 180 degrees

Dribbling in a star (180-degree turn)
The coach gives a signal and the players dribble simultaneously from the outside cones to the center cone. One yard from the center they drag the ball back and dribble back to the outside cones.

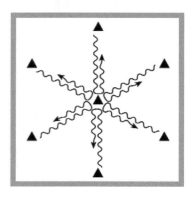

Possible techniques:
- Drag back with the sole of the foot
- Change of direction with the inside of the foot
- Change of direction with the outside of the foot

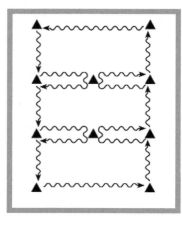

Basic techniques in a comb

The players dribble round the given comb path (forward - to the middle - backward - forward - etc.) using the following techniques:
- Drag back with the sole of the foot
- Change of direction with the inside of the foot
- Change of direction with the outside of the foot

This gives the players the confidence on the ball that they need when an opponent challenges from the side. They learn to use certain techniques automatically to shield the ball and dribble away from the opponent.

Change of direction with the outside of the foot

Techniques in the comb - groups of 2

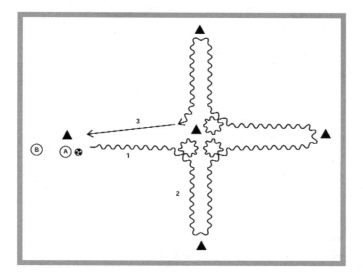

The players practice the change of direction through 180 degrees in groups of 2.
(1) A dribbles to the first cone.
(2) A carries out alternate 90-degree and 180-degree turns
(3) After A has dribbled round the course he/she plays the ball to B.

Drills with an opponent

A dribbles toward the center cone. B challenges from the right. A turns his/her back to B and takes the ball backward with a specified technique (drag back with the sole, change of direction with the inside of the foot, change of direction with the outside of the foot).

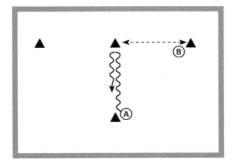
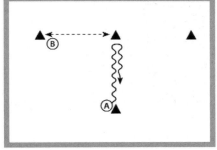

When both players are back at the starting cone they start again. After 5 rounds to the right and left sides the players swap roles. A becomes the defender and B dribbles.

E) End game
- Burnout (game W1 - game time: 2 x 7 minutes
- Two goals

PRACTICE SESSION D 4
DRIBBLING FOLLOWED BY A TASK

A) Setting the mood
Warm-up games: G9 - Hunters and hares and /or G15 - Surprise tag

B) Warm-up drill: Dribbling in a triangle
Each player sets up a triangle and dribbles from cone to cone. After each round he/she changes the turning direction.

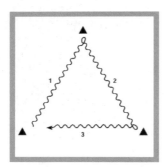

Possible techniques:
- Change of direction with the inside of the foot
- Change of direction with the outside of the foot
- Turn through 270 degrees with the inside of the foot

C) Coordination conditioning
Zipper drills (see pp. 94, 95) without a ball.

D) Main phase
Drills in groups of 3
One player dribbles round a course and plays the ball to the outside player, who returns it immediately. After an agreed time the players swap roles. The coach explains how to pull the ball behind the standing leg and the players practice this intensively in the drill along with other already familiar techniques.

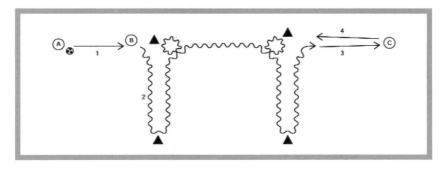

(1) A plays the ball to B.

(2) B takes the ball to the side and carried out a 180-degree turn at the next cone.

(3) At the end of the course he/she plays the ball to C.

(4) C plays the ball back immediately to B, who dribbles back.

Techniques
Change of direction with the inside of the foot, drag-back and behind the standing leg (new).

Comb drills - group of 3

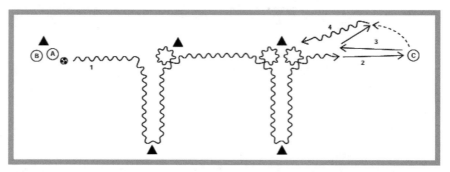

(1) A dribbles round the course (as in the previous drill).
(2) At the end of the course A plays the ball to C.
(3) C plays a one-touch pass back to A, who plays the ball to the side with his/her first touch and takes over the position of C.
(4) C takes the pass and dribbles round the course.

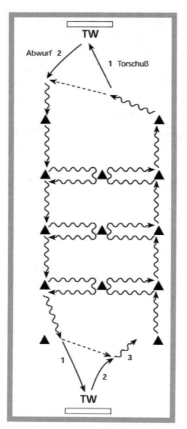

Techniques in the comb with shot at goal
In this drill the players combine the techniques they have learned with a shot at goal. This has the advantage that there are no long waiting times (files) and the players have to carry out a movement before they shoot.

E) End game
- Catch the dribbler (game W3).
- Game with 4 goals.

PRACTICE SESSION D 5
FIGURE-EIGHT DRIBBLING

A) Setting the mood
Warm-up games: G12 - Six-day race and/or G6 - Characteristics

B) Warm-up drill: Comb
The coach sets up the comb for groups of 4. The players start at 2 cones and dribble in the given pattern. When the coach calls, the players switch to another technique (drag-back with the sole, change of direction with the inside or outside of the foot, drag behind the standing leg, etc.).

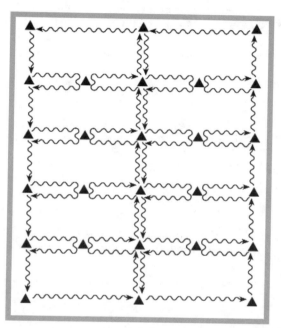

Comb for group of 4

C) Coordination conditioning
Zipper drills (see page 95)

D) Main phase: Dribbling for more advanced players
Taking the ball past an opponent in front
After a dummy step, the players (A1 and B1) pass the ball to the waiting players (A2 and B2).

Figure-of-eight dribbling in groups of 3
The players repeat the following techniques in the new practice setup:
Change of direction with inside of foot, turning through 270 degrees with inside of foot, dragging the ball behind the standing leg.
(1) A dribbles to the first cone.
(2) Figure-of-eight dribbles: Diagonal forward - back - diagonal forward.

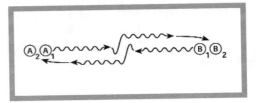

(3) A passes to C and takes up his/her position (4).
(5) C takes the pass and dribbles in the same way round the course.

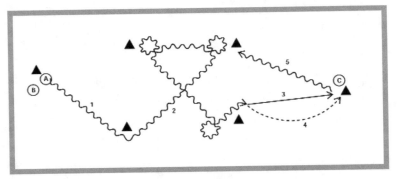

(6) C dribbles diagonally forward - back - diagonally forward.
(7) C passes the ball to B and swaps positions with him/her (8).

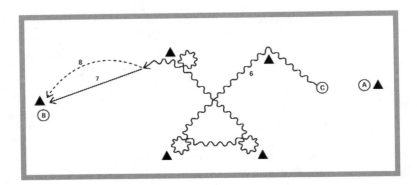

Figure-of-eight dribbling with shot at goal

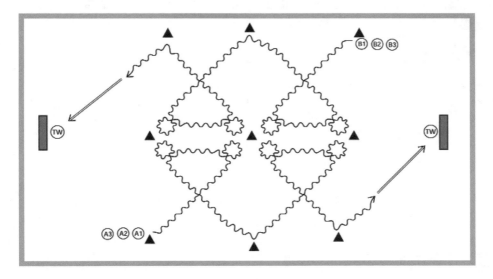

E) End game
• Dribblers versus juggler (game W7)
• Game with 2 goals
The five practice sessions in this series can be used a s a basis for further practice sessions. Simply combine content, coaching setups and games, so that the players practice the important basic movements in new constellations.

Series 2: Taking a pass and running with the ball

Passing movements with a second player, creating openings for shots at goal and neat build-up play require different techniques to be used for kicking the ball and taking a pass and running with the ball. The high speed of modern soccer gives the players no opportunity to stop the ball and then carry out a follow-up action. Rather, it is essential for the first touch to lead straight into the next action when a player takes a pass.

Notes on the method
• In the first phase the players practice controlling low passes with their first touch before running with the ball (inside of foot/outside of foot).
• The movements of controlling the ball and running with it should flow smoothly into each other; the first touch should lead into the run.

PRACTICE SESSION A 1
TAKING A PASS WITH THE INSIDE OF THE FOOT AND RUNNING WITH THE BALL

A) Setting the mood / warming up

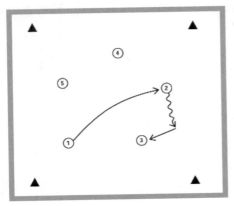

Numbers game
- Five players in one group are num
  bered from 1 to 5. Player 1 has the
  ball.
- All players move freely in the playing area.
- Player 1 passes to player 2. Player 2
  takes the ball and runs with it for a
  short distance, then passes to 3, and
  so on.

B) Warm-up drill
- Zigzag in a group of 3
- Repetition of taking a pass and running with the ball after the zigzag and
  the acquired dribbling techniques.

C) Coordination conditioning
Running and jumping drills in a triangle of rods (see pp. 94, 95).

D) Main phase: Taking a low pass with the inside of the foot and running with the ball

Drill 1: Running diagonally forward with the ball
- A and B stand 3 to 5 yards apart.
- A passes to B, who takes the ball with
  the inside of the foot and runs diagonally forward.
- B passes to A and runs back to the
  cone.

Number: Ten repetitions taking the pass
with the right foot and running left and taking it with the left foot and running right. The players then change their positions.

Drill 2: Taking a pass with the inside of the foot and running to the side

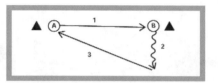

- B plays a low pass to A, who takes it with the inside of the foot and runs to the side (90 degrees).
- A dribbles back and passes the ball low to B.
- B takes the pass with the inside of the foot and runs to the side.

And so on.

Drill 3: Taking a pass and turning and running away from the passer

A takes a low pass from B with the inside of the foot and turns away from the passer and runs with the ball.

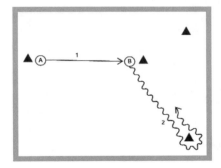

Drill 4:
The players walk/run toward the ball before running forward, to the side or backward.

Drill 5:
The players feint to sprint to the opposite side before taking the pass and running with it.

Drill 6:
Taking and pass and running with the ball in groups of 3
- Four cones are set up as shown in the illustration.
- The passers stand beside the outside cones.
- Player C stands beside one of the inside cones, waiting for the first pass from A.
- He/she takes the pass with the inside of the foot and dribbles to the second inside cone.
- He/she then passes to B, who plays the ball with his/her first touch to C.
- The next take and run sequence follows.
- After 10 take and run sequences the players swap roles.

E) End
Games with just one goal and a goalkeeper (see pp. 64-66).

PRACTICE SESSION A 2
TAKING A PASS WITH THE OUTSIDE OF THE FOOT AND RUNNING WITH THE BALL

A) Setting the mood
Warm-up games: G8 - Island hopping and/or G4 - Fruit salad

B) Warm-up drill
Pairs of players repeat the first drill of practice session A1.

C) Coordination conditioning
Running and jumping drills in a triangle of tires and rods (see pp. 94, 95).

D) Main phase: Taking a low pass with the outside of the foot and running with the ball

Drill 1: Taking a pass with the outside of the foot and running to the side with the ball
• A and B stand facing each other 5 yards apart.
• A takes a low pass from B with the outside of his/her foot and turns through 90 degrees and runs with the ball.
• He/she then dribbles back and passes low to B, who also takes the pass with the outside of the foot and turns through 90 degrees and runs with the ball.

Number: 10 repeats taking the ball with the right foot to the right and 10 repeats taking the ball with the left foot to the left.

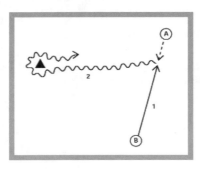

Drill 2: Walking/running to meet the ball
- A walks or runs to meet the ball and take it with the outside of the foot and turn through 90 degrees.
- He/she dribbles round the cone and passes to B.
- Ten repeats with the right foot and 10 repeats with the left.

Drill 3: Taking a pass, turning and running diagonally away from the passer

- A and B stand facing each other 5 to 7 yards apart. B passes to A (1), who moves to meet the ball. A takes the pass, turns and runs diagonally away from B.
- A dribbles round the cone (2), passes back to B and runs back to his/her original position.
- After 10 repeats the players change roles.

Drill 4: Taking a pass and running with the ball in a square
- A and B stand facing each other 6 to 8 yards apart.
- A passes low to B, who moves to meet the ball, takes it with the outside of the foot, turns through 90 degrees and runs with the ball.
- A runs parallel to B. At the other side of the square they turn to face each other again.
- B passes to A, and so on.

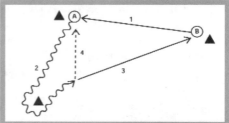

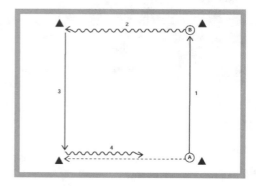

Drill 5: Taking a pass and running with ball in a square in groups of 3

(1) A passes to B and sprints after the ball.
(2) B takes the pass and runs with the ball to the free cone.
(3) B passes to C and sprints after the ball.
(4) C takes the pass and runs with the ball to the free cone.
(5) C passes to A, and so on.

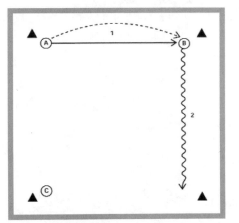
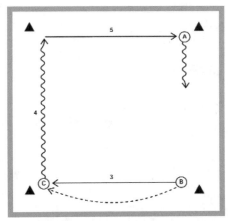

When each player is back in his/her original position, the players repeat the sequence in the opposite direction. A then passes first to C, etc.

E) End game

• Kings and soldiers (game W16)
• Game with 2 goals.

Series 3: Juggling

A player needs a good feel for the ball and excellent coordination to keep a ball in the air with foot, thigh, head, shoulders, etc. without allowing it to fall to the ground. It takes a lot of practice to acquire a feeling for the right amount of strength to use and the right moment to play the ball into the air. The ball reacts immediately to the smallest error (e.g. wrong timing, or use of too much or too little strength) and falls out of the player's reach. If a beginner plays the ball too high, he/she will have problems with the next ball contact, as the ball falls faster and is harder to control. Beginners should learn the basic ball juggling skills step by step. These basics enable players to practice further in their own time. With regular practice, players learn to keep the ball in the air in a controlled manner with the foot, thigh, etc.

Why is juggling important for a young player's soccer development?
- Juggling promotes agility and dexterity in dealing with the ball.
- It develops a feel for the ball, without which good ball technique is impossible.
- The player learns to coordinate his/her movements with those of the ball.

Notes on the method
- Juggling must not become an aim in itself. It should be embedded in the development process of young soccer players. The pace of modern soccer is so fast that there is no place for pure ball jugglers.
- Elements of juggling can be incorporated in drills for individuals and groups of 2 or 3
- Players must be given sufficient opportunities to practice intensively with a ball on their own. They must be able to play the ball with both the right and left foot.

- When players can handle a ball with a certain degree of competence, they can practice in groups.
- It is advisable to allow the players to practice together in a limited area from the very start. In this way they learn to focus simultaneously on the ball, the ball path, the area around them and the other players.

Aims of juggling practice

- Juggling with both feet
- Sequences of juggling actions with few or no ground contacts.
- Encouragement of creativity through variable use of foot, thigh, chest and head. In individual practice the players should systematically increase the number of ball contacts with various parts of the body.

Juggling is very demanding

- Coordination
- Special soccer techniques (playing the ball into the air)
- Mobility
- Concentration
- Balance (ability to stand securely on one leg)

PRACTICE SESSION J I
BASIC DRILLS

A) Setting the mood - Warming up
Warm-up games:
G11 - Pickpocket and/or G16 - Dribbling through the goal

B) Warm-up drill
Repetition of techniques in zigzag for groups of 4.

C) Coordination conditioning
Drills in tire course followed by a final task (see pp. 98, 99).

D) Main phase: Juggling - basic drills
These basic drills familiarize the players with playing the ball into the air with various parts of the body. This is simplest when the ball is dropped from the hand or thrown up a short distance into the air.

Individual drills
Drill 1: Drop the ball / thigh
- Drop the ball and propel it into the air with the thigh and catch it again.
- Number of repetitions: 10 with the right thigh, 10 with the left thigh, 10 with right and left alternately
- Steadily increase the height.

Drill 2: Throw the ball up / thigh
- Throw the ball up. As it falls, propel it into the air with the thigh and catch it again.

- Number of repetitions: 10 with the right thigh, 10 with the left thigh, 10 with right and left alternately

Drill 3: Throw the ball up / forehead
- Hold the ball in both hands and throw it up 18 inches above head height
- Head the falling ball up and catch it.
- Repeat 10 times.

Drill 4: Drop the ball / instep
- Drop the ball or throw it a short distance into the air.
- Before the ball bounces, kick it into the air with the instep and catch it.
- Number of repetitions: 10 with the right foot, 10 with the left foot, 10 with right and left alternately

Drill 5: Drop the ball / bounce / instep
- Throw the ball vertically into the air. Allow it to bounce, then catch it.
- Throw the ball into the air. Allow it to bounce, then kick it into the air with the instep and catch it.
- After each bounce, kick the ball as high as possible with the instep.

E) End games
- Runaround (game W5)
- Game with 2 teams.

PRACTICE SESSION J 2
INDIVIDUAL DRILLS FOR MORE ADVANCED PLAYERS

A) Setting the mood
Warm-up games:
G13 - Hundred point dribble and/or G7 - Dribbling by numbers

B) Warm-up drill: Juggling with ground contact
- The players juggle the ball inside a marked area. After each contact the ball is allowed to bounce.
- The coach observes how securely the players can keep the ball in the air. He/she helps players who have problems playing the ball into the air (ball height and direction).
- Advanced players practice more advanced techniques.

C) Coordination conditioning
Drills in rod course with give-and-go.

D) Main phase: Individual drills for advanced players

Drill 1: Combinations with catching
- The player combines 2 contacts with the thigh, head and foot in a given sequence and then catches the ball:
- "foot-head" or "foot-thigh"
- "thigh-head" or "thigh-foot"
- "head-thigh" or "head-foot"
- The player combines 3 contacts with thigh, head and foot in a given sequence:
- "foot-thigh-head"

Drill 2: Juggling with ground contact while moving forward
- Kick the ball in the air with the instep while moving forward.
- Allow the ball to bounce once after each contact.

Drill 3: Juggling without ball contact
The player juggles the ball with the instep, head, chest or thigh as long as he/she can:
- With the instep (only right/only left/right and left alternately)
- With the thigh (only right/only left/right and left alternately)
- With the head
- Free juggling with instep, thigh and head
- Specified combinations with instep, thigh and head
  - "instep-thigh"
  - "instep-head"
  - "instep-thigh-head"

If the ball falls to the ground, the player lifts it into the air with the foot. He/she rolls the ball back under the sole, giving it sufficient motion to roll onto the instep or the front of the foot. In one movement he/she lifts the ball up with the foot and starts to juggle it.

E) End: Soccer tennis tournament without net - one against one
This game helps players to improve their juggling technique. It promotes concentration and is a lot of fun (see game W6, pp. 41-43)
- Ball allowed to bounce
- Ball not allowed to bounce

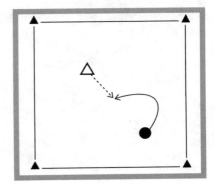

PRACTICE SESSION J3
DRILLS IN GROUPS OF 2 OR MORE

Introduction
It is useful to incorporate playing a ball into the air in a controlled and carefully weighted manner in a group situation. This introduces the necessary
variation, and thus motivation and concentration, into the "battle against
gravity." The players must have mastered the basic juggling skills they practiced in individual drills.

A) Setting the mood
Dribblers versus jugglers (game W7, pp. 43-45)

B) Warm-up drill
Warm-up drill
Repetition of juggling techniques without ground contact
The coach observes and advises.

C) Coordination conditioning
Drills in rod and tire course with header as final task.

D) Main phase: Drills for groups of 2 and more
Drill 1: Drop the ball / pass with instep
- Two players stand facing each other 3 to 5 yards apart and play the ball
  back and forth with the instep.
- The receiver takes the ball on the thigh, chest or head.
- He/she then picks up the ball, drops it and volleys it with the instep to the
  other player.

Drill 2: Pass without catch

- The players play the ball back and forth with the instep.
- The receiver takes the ball on the thigh or chest.
- He/she passes the ball back without using his/her hands
- The players must always face each other full on.

Variation: Before the player passes the ball back, he/she juggles a few times with the foot, thigh and head.

Drill 3: Juggling in a group

- The first player passes with the instep to the player opposite, runs after the ball and joins the opposite group.
- The next player takes the pass, runs a short distance, juggles with the ball briefly (2 or 3 contacts) and plays the ball back to the other side.

Note

When receiving a pass and juggling, the players should get their body behind the ball.

Drill 4: Juggling in a circle
- One player is in the middle of the circle.
- The players forming the circle play the ball back to the player in the middle.

Phase 1: The player in the middle throws the ball to one of the others, who controls it, juggles it briefly (2 or 3 contacts) and returns it.

Phase 2: The player in the middle does not catch the return pass but takes it on his/her chest, thigh, foot or head and volleys it to another player.

E) End games
- Soccer tennis tournament - 2 against 2 without a net (see game W6, pp. 41-43).
- 4 against 4 tournament

The teams for the 4 against 4 tournament are formed from 8 pairs of players on the basis of the results of the soccer tennis tournament (1st and 8th pairs, 2nd and 7th, 3rd and 6th, 4th and 5th).

Series 4: Passing - give-and-go

The first 2 practice sessions (P 1 and P 2 deal with the basics of passing, while the practice sessions P3 to P 5 deal with the double pass

PRACTICE SESSION P I
FACE-TO-FACE PASSING

A) Setting the mood
Warm-up game: G14 - Greetings and/or G2 - Plague in Venice

B) Warm-up drill
Repetition of the warm-up drills in the comb

C) Coordination conditioning
Soccer-specific coordination drills with an additional task (see p. 80)

D) Main phase: Face-to-face passing

Drill I: Stationary passing in groups of 2
Description:
- The players stand facing each other 5 to 10 yards apart.
- Between them is a goal (1 to 2 yards wide).
- A plays the stationary ball from a standing position with the inside of the foot (toes pointing to the side) so that it passes through the goal on its way to B.
- B takes the ball on the inside of the foot and passes it back through the goal to A.

Notes
- The passer looks at the other player before striking the ball.
- The width of the goal can be reduced if the players can pass accurately.
- The speed of the passing sequence should be gradually increased.
- The distance between the players should be steadily increased.
- The players should practice with both the left and right foot.

Drill 2: Running to meet the pass
Before the passer strikes the ball, the other player walks or runs a few steps to meet the ball. The distance between the players should be steadily increased.

Drill 3: Varying the distance
The players strike the ball with the inside of the foot while on the move. They continuously shorten and lengthen their distance apart from 2 to 3 yards to 10 to 12 yards.

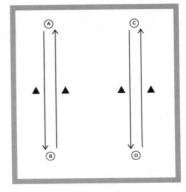

Drill 4: Fixed passer
The passer (X) passes to the first player in the line, who returns it with his/her first touch and joins the back of the line.
Note: This drill can also be used competitively. The team that can play the ball back and forth the most times in 1 minute is the winner.

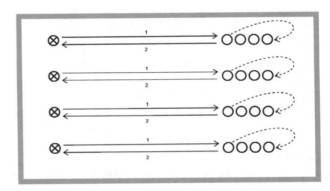

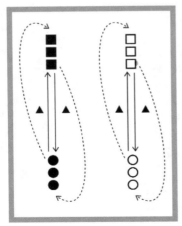

Drill 5: Continuous drills with 5 players
The players pass the ball between the cones with their first or second touch and join the back of the other group.

E) End
• Dribbling versus technique (passing game) (see W8).
• Game with 2 goals. Only 2 (or 3) ball contacts are allowed. This prevents the players from dribbling and encourages them to pass the ball.

PRACTICE SESSION P 2
PASSING TO THE SIDE

A) Setting the mood
Warm-up game: G4 - Fruit salad and/or G10 - Shield the ball

B) Warm-up drill
The players pass the ball through the goals, run round the cones and take up position on the other side.

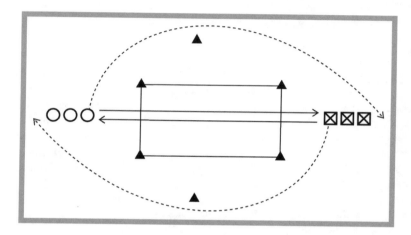

C) Coordination conditioning
Soccer-specific coordination drills - weighted passing game (see p. 80).

D) Main phase: Passing to the side

Drill 1: Passing in a triangle
The players pass the ball clockwise with the inside of the foot to the next player in the triangle. The passer runs after the ball to the next player's position.

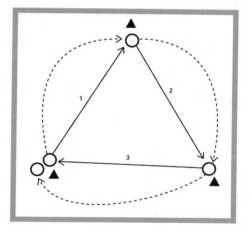

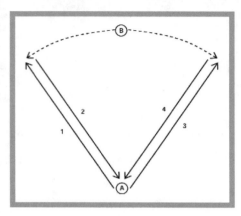

Drill 2: Passing on the run - 1 ball
- A plays the ball low to the right and left alternately.
- B runs back and forth and plays the ball back to A with the right and left foot alternately.

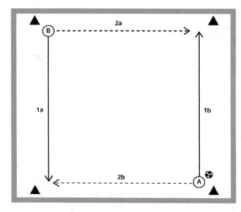

Drill 3: Passing on the run - 2 balls
- A and B stand diagonally opposite each other.
- At the same moment, each player plays his/her ball along one side of the square. Each player runs to receive the other player's pass.
- They then play the balls back simultaneously.

Note: The players must look at each other just before playing the ball.

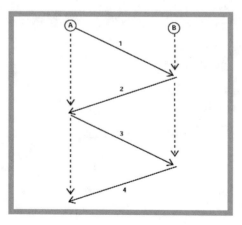

4: Passing on the run
- The players run forward in parallel straight lines, 4 to 6 yards apart.
- Each player passes with the inside of the foot to the other while on the run.

Drill 5: Short-long-short (1 ball)

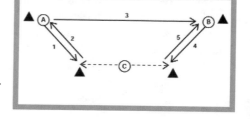

The player in the middle (C) runs back and forth between the 2 cones and plays short passes to the other 2 players.

(1) A plays the ball into the path of C.
(2) C passes back to A with his/her first touch and sprints to the other cone.
(3) A plays a long pass to B.
(4) B plays a short pass to C.
(5) C returns the ball with his/her first touch and sprints to the other cone. B plays a long pass to A and the sequence then starts again.

E) End

• Flatball (game W9)
• Game of 4 against 4 in a square with 2 neutral players on the sidelines.

PRACTICE SESSION P 3
BASICS OF GIVE-AND-GO

Preliminary comments on give-and-go

Definition: Give-and-go

A give-and-go is a sequence of two passes, with which the ball is taken past an opponent. A runner passes to a teammate, sprints past the opponent and runs onto the return pass. It is also referred to as a wall pass, and the player who makes the return pass is sometimes referred to as the wall player. Both passes must be played in such a way that the opponent cannot intercept them. After receiving the return pass the runner can sprint into the free space behind the opponent.

A successful give-and-go depends on:

• precision passing by both the runner and the wall player
• correct timing

Passing techniques for give-and-go:

• Pass with the inside of the foot
• Pass with the inside instep
• Pass with the outside instep

Passing with the inside of the foot is the basic technique for accurate short passing. A "camouflaged" pass to the wall player with the outside instep and

a return pass with the inside or outside instep have a greater element of surprise for the opposing defense but are technically more demanding and risky.
In the first session the players practice accurate passing in various configura-
tions.

A) Setting the mood
Warm-up games: G1 Simon says and/or G12 - Six-day race

B) Warm-up drill: Passing game in groups of 4
A successful give-and-go in a game situation is only possible if the players
can pass precisely on the run. Each group of 4 (or 5) has one ball.

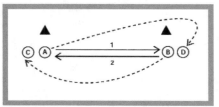

(1) A plays the ball to B and immediately runs to the other side.
(2) B plays the ball with his/her first
touch to B and also switches sides.
The passing sequence is continued until
the coach ends it (5 minutes).

C) Coordination conditioning
Drills to improve coordination and technique, with an additional task (see
pp. 98, 99).

D) Main phase: Passing
Drill I
(1) A sidefoots the stationary ball low to B (distance apart 5 to 8 yards).
(2) B walks/runs from the cone in the direction of the ball and sidefoots it
back low with his/her first touch.
(3) B sprints round his/her cone and waits for the next pass from A.

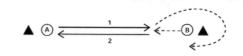

Passing game in groups of 2 - a player
runs to meet the ball

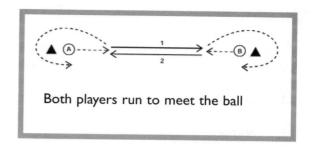

Both players run to meet the ball

Drill 2

Two marker cones are set up 10 to 15 yards apart.
Players A and B stand in front of the cones.
(1) A plays the ball to B, who runs to meet it.
(2) B passes the ball with his/her first touch back to A and sprints round his/her cone.
(3) A also runs to meet the ball, plays it back to B with his/her first touch and sprints round his/her cone.

Game A: Give-and-go

Goals are set up in an arc of 20 to 30 yards. There is one goal for each pair of players. The goal is 1.5 to 2 yards wide. The goals are marked by cones or flagpoles. A player from group A stands in each goal. The players of group B stand in the middle with one ball.

Phase 1:

• The players of group B run with a ball within the circle. The players of group A serve as wall players.
• Each player in the circle dribbles toward a goal and passes on the run to the player standing in the goal, who plays a return pass into his/her path. The player from group B then dribbles to the next free goal.
• The team B players score one point for each give-and-go.

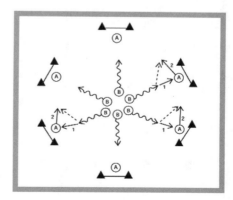

Practicing give-and-go

Note

The coach should ensure that the runners:
- Look at the wall player before passing to him/her
- Pass the ball low, hard and accurately to the feet of the wall player
- Run into free space to the side immediately after passing.

The wall player should return the ball precisely into the path of the runner

Main elements

- Improving one-touch passing between runners and wall players
- Improving passing and running into space (runners)
- Improving running into space and one-touch passing (wall players)
- Improving the timing of the actions of the runners and wall players
- Executing give-and-gos

Who wins?

- The runner who scores the most points in an agreed time is the winner.
- The runner who reaches an agreed number of points in the shortest time is the winner.

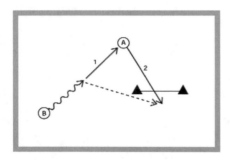

Phase 2

- The wall player is 1 or 2 yards behind the goal.
- The runner passes the ball to the right or left of the goal.
- The wall player returns the ball through the goal.

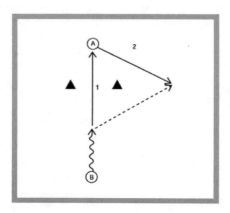

Phase 3

- The wall player is 1 or 2 yards behind the goal.
- The runner passes the ball through the goal.
- The wall player returns the ball to the right or left of the goal.

E) Warming-down
- Game with 2 goals (additional rule: goals after a give-and-go count double)

PRACTICE UNIT P 4
CONTINUOUS DRILLS WITH GIVE-AND-GO

A) Setting the mood
Warm-up game: G5 - Shadow dribbling and/or G15 - Surprise tag

B) Warm-up drill: Passing in a triangle
Two players stand at each of the 3 cones marking a triangle. The cones are 6 to 10 yards apart. A has a ball, passes it to B, sprints after it and stands behind B. B passes with his/her first touch to C and runs to stands behind C.

C passes to A, and so on.
Minimum number of players: 4 (2 players at the starting position and 1 player at each of the other cones).

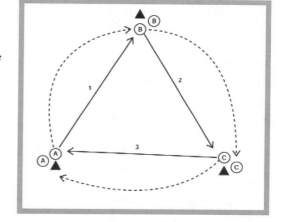

Variations for more advanced players
Run in the opposite direction: Play the ball to the right and run to the left.
- A passes to B and runs to stand behind C.
- B passes to C and runs to stand behind A.
- C passes to A and runs to stand behind B.

C) Coordination conditioning
Drills with the coordination ladder.

D) Main phase: Improving give-and-go play
Continuous format A: Two permanent wall players (large group)
Half of the players stand at each cone with a ball. The distance between cones is 15 to 25 yards, depending on the size of the group. In the middle are 2 wall players. At a sign from the coach the first player of each group starts off on a short dribble followed by a give and go. After taking the return pass the 2 players run on and join the opposite group. After one minute the wall players are replaced, so that each player can practice playing give-and-gos while running with the ball.

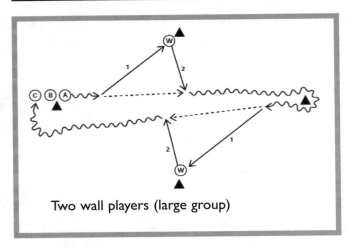

Two wall players (large group)

Variation: Focus on the wall player

To put pressure on the wall player, 2 cones are set up 1 yard apart. After the give-and-go at the first cone, the wall player runs round the second cone and back to the first one. The next player passes to him/her just before he/she arrives back at the first cone. After 10 passes the wall player is replaced.

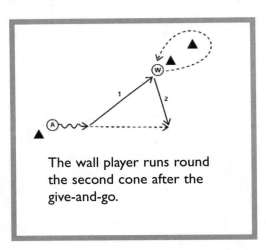

The wall player runs round the second cone after the give-and-go.

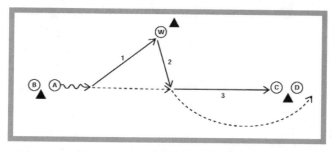

Continuous format B: One wall player (small groups)

The coach forms groups of 5 to 6 players. Two or three players stand at the cones, which are 15 yards apart, and a wall player stands in the middle.
(1) A passes diagonally to the wall player, who plays a one-touch pass back into A's path.
(2) A plays a one-touch pass to C.
(3) C plays a give-and-go with the wall player either with his/her first touch or after a short dribble.

Variation: Focus on the wall player

• The wall player sprints round a second cone before playing the next pass.
• An opponent challenges the wall player during the give-and-go without actually trying to take the ball. The wall player thus comes under pressure and must shield the ball.

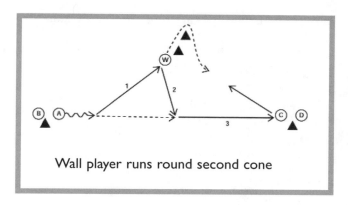

Wall player runs round second cone

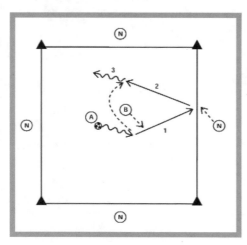

Game of 1 against 1 plus 4 neutral players
Two players play against each other in the square. The four neutral players are available as wall players. Numerous give-and-go situations arise. The playing time should be no more than 1 minute, as the game is very strenuous.

E) Warming-down

- Game with 2 goals (additional rule: a goal after a give-and-go counts double).

PRACTICE SESSION P 5
THE GIVE-AND-GO IN COMPETITIVE GAMES

A) Setting the mood
Warm-up game:
G8 - Island hopping and/or G10 - Shield the ball

B) Warm-up drill: Passing game in a circle
Five to seven players stand in a circle with a diameter of 8 to 12 yards. A plays the first pass across the circle to E and runs after the ball. The passer takes over the position of the player who receives the pass.
Variation: The player who receives the ball runs to meet it and plays it on the run (see drawing).

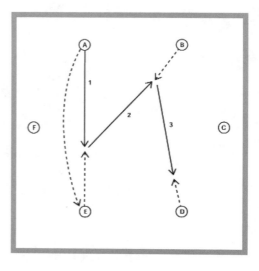

C) Coordination conditioning
Drills with the coordination ladder.

D) Main phase: Competitive give-and-go
Game format: Give-and-go followed by fast dribble.
The players dribble at a relaxed pace in an area marked with cones (40 x 40 yards). Five wall players are available to participate in give-and-gos.

Game rules
- The players (A) in possession of a ball play give-and-gos with the 5 wall players. Each passer seeks a free wall player.
- After the give-and-go, he/she dribbles quickly out of the marked area and round a cone before seeking another free wall player.
- Each give-and-go combined with a dribble round an outside cone scores one point for the dribbler.

Who wins?
- The player who scores most points in an agreed time is the winner.
- The player who scores an agreed number of points in the shortest time is the winner.

Variation
The first and second pass of the give-and-go must be carried out with a specified technique (inside of foot, inside instep, outside instep).

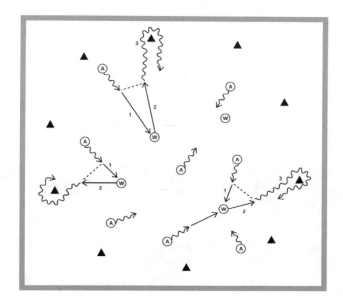

Drills in Pairs:

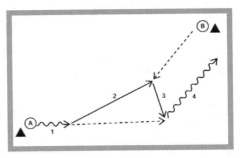

Sprint to the ball - pass on the run - give-and-go
A dribbles with the ball. B runs toward A, who passes diagonally into B's path. B plays a one-touch pass back to A. A dribbles to B's cone. The players swap roles and repeat the sequence.

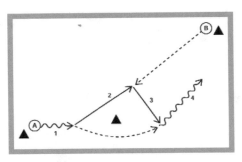

Taking the ball past a passive opponent (cone) with a give-and-go
A cone is set up to represent an opponent. This forces the players to play the give-and-go at a defined position.

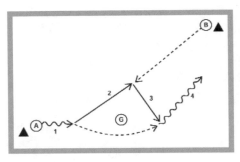

Taking the ball past a semi-active opponent
An opponent is now introduced into the game. The opponent challenges the player who runs with the ball (see photo).

- After the give-and-go the runner and the wall player swap roles.
- The opponent is replaced after 10 give-and-gos.

Pressure on the wall player - taking the ball past an opponent
A dribbles toward opponent G1 and keeps his/her eye on the wall player, who makes a sudden spurt and calls for the ball.
- A plays the ball into the path of B, who is semi-actively challenged by opponent G2.
- A sprints past opponent G1 and takes the return pass from B.
- A and B swap positions.
- After 10 sequences the players swap roles.

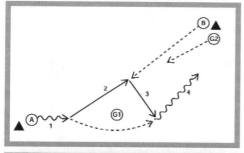

Give-and-go with 2 players

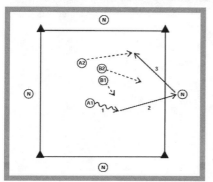

Two against two + 4 neutral players

E) Warming-down
- Game with 4 goals (additional rule: goals after a give-and-go count double)

Series 5: Heading

The header is often neglected in the coaching of young soccer players, although the players have to defend against high balls, head crosses at goal, etc. Heading technique should be taught from the very beginning. Coaches should, however, plan such this carefully and take the following points into consideration:

- A light ball should be used.
- The players should head the ball with the forehead.
- The practice phases should be short.
- Throwers, passers, headers and goalkeepers should swap roles frequently.
- The ball should not be thrown or passed over long distances.

Note: The swingball is a suitable aid for coaching heading technique. This is attached to the crossbar and has a short swing. The players stand inside the goal.

Swingball

PRACTICE SESSION H I
BASICS (DRILLS FOR 2 PLAYERS)

The following steps teach young players how to head the ball straight ahead and to one side.
• Header while standing still
• Header while walking to meet the ball
• Header while running slowly to meet the ball
• Header while running fast to met the ball

A) Setting the mood
Warm-up game: G2 - Plague in Venice and/or G14 - Greetings

B) Warm-up drill
Four or five players stand in a circle and head the ball to each other. Beginners catch the ball in their hands, throw it in the air and head it to the next player.

C) Coordination conditioning
Headers in the coordination ladder.

D) Main phase
Drill I: Header while standing still
• The players stand 3 to 5 yards apart.
• A throws the ball into the air and heads it to B.
• B catches the ball and heads it back in the same way.

Note
The older and more practiced the young players are, the greater the distance apart should be.

Drill 2: Header directly back to the thrower
• A throws the ball to B.
• B heads the ball to A so that he/she can catch it.
• After 5 throws the players swap roles - B throws and A heads.

Drill 3: Header directly back and forth
• The players try to head the ball 10 times back and forth.

Drill 4: Header while running forward
• A moves backward and throws the ball to B.
• B runs forward and heads the ball back so that A can catch it.
• After the players have moved 10 to 15 yards they return to their starting positions. A throws and B heads.

Drill 5: Header to the side while standing still
• A throws the ball to B and runs to the side.
• B heads the ball to B so that he/she can catch it.
• After 5 headers the players swap roles.
• The upper body should turn in the new direction before the player heads the ball.

Drill 6: Header to the side while running
• A lobs the ball to B so that it falls to one side.
• B runs to the side and heads the ball back to A.
• After 5 headers the players swap roles.
• The more practiced the players are, the further the ball can be thrown to the side.

Drill 7: Header while running forward
• The players run forward parallel to each other, 5 yards apart.
• A throws the ball in the path of B.
• B heads the ball back into A's path, so that A can catch it.
• A throws the ball again to B, who heads it back again. The sequence is repeated until the players have covered the given distance (20 yards).

E) End game: Handball headers (game W12)
Game rules
• Two teams and 2 goals.
• The players throw the ball to each other.
• Goals can only be scored with headers.
• Players can only defend the goal by heading the ball.

PRACTICE SESSION H 2
HEADERS IN GROUPS OF THREE

A) Warm-up game: Handball - headers
This game is suitable for both warming down and warming up.

B) Warm-up drill
The players practice passing, taking the ball and running with it, and dribbling in a complex pattern.
(1) A1 passes to B and runs after the ball, then turns and waits for the next pass.
(2) B takes the ball and runs with it briefly, then passes to C and runs after the ball.
(3) C passes to D and also runs after the ball.
(4) D takes the ball and dribbles round the course, using various dribbling techniques.

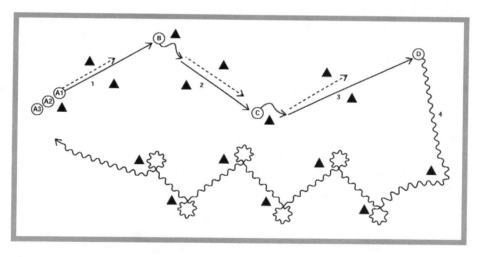

C) Coordination conditioning
Coordination and technique - headers after throw in the rod course
The players work in groups of 2. They are given 2 hurdles or rods, which they lay parallel on the ground. One player throws the ball and the other heads it. After running fast sideways over the rods, the player heads the ball back to his/her partner.

D) Main phase: Headers in groups of three

The players are given 2 balls. Two players throw the ball alternately to the third player, who heads them back to the throwers.

Drill 1: 2 balls - slight turn

- A and B each throw a ball to C, who turns slightly and heads the ball back so that the thrower can catch it.

Drill 2: 2 balls - slight turn while running forward

- A and B move back, and C heads the ball while running forward.

Drill 3: 2 balls - big turn

- A, B and C stand in a line.
- A and B each hold a ball.
- C is in the middle between A and B.
- A throws the ball to C, who heads it back and then turns to face B.
- B throws the ball to C, who heads it back.
- After 10 headers the players swap roles.

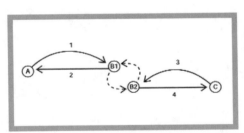

Variation

The players A and C throw the ball straight up in the air and head it to B.

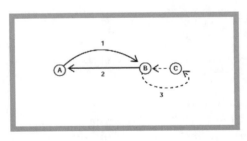

Drill 5: 1 ball - A throws - B and C change

- A, B and C stand in a line.
- A is the thrower.
- B and C stand in line. They take turns to head the ball back to A, moving to the back after each header.

Drill 6: I ball - defensive header

- A throws the ball
- B and C jump. B heads the ball and C challenges B.
- C heads back to A.
- After 5 to 10 headers the players change positions.

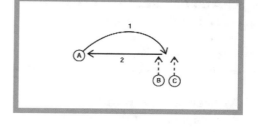

Drill 7: I ball - header and turn

In this drill the players practice heading the ball while turning. The throw-head-throw sequence changes constantly.

- A throws to B, who heads to C.
- C catches the ball and throws to A, who heads to B.
- B catches and throws to C, who heads to A, and so on.

Variations

- Jumping and heading
- Diving header

E) End game: Handball - headers (4 against 4)

The players try to throw the ball into the goal area and head it into goal. Inside the goal area the ball can only be headed. There is no goalkeeper. If the ball falls to the ground, an opponent picks it up and returns it into play.

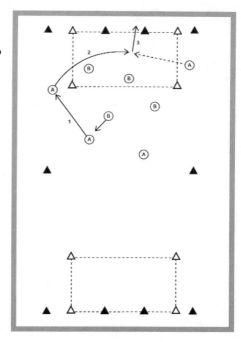

PRACTICE SESSION H 3
HEADING AT GOAL

After the basic heading drills, in this practice session the players use heading techniques in goalscoring and other game situations.

A) Setting the mood
Warm-up games: G3 - Grand prix and/or G9 - Hunters and hares

B) Warm-up drill
The players repeat the comb techniques:
• Drag-back under the sole
• Change of direction with the inside of the foot
• Change of direction with the outside of the foot

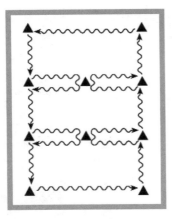

C) Coordination conditioning
Coordination drills with the coordination ladder (see pp. 100 -105)

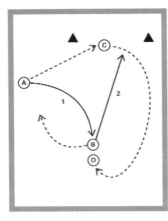

D) Main phase: Headers at goal

Drill 1: Throw and header at goal
• A throws the ball in an arc to B.
• B runs to meet the ball and heads it at goal.
• C tries to catch or stop the ball.
• The players then swap roles. A goes into goal, C fetches the ball and runs to stand behind D. B becomes the thrower.
• D heads the second ball.
• Variation: Jump and header

Game "From goal to goal"

- The players set up 2 goals 4 to 7 yards apart.
- Player A stands on one goal line, throws the ball straight up into the air and tries to head the ball into the opposite goal.
- The height of the goal is the height of the players.
- 1 point is awarded for a goal.

Notes

- The coach organizes a small tournament.
- Each player plays 5 times against different opponents chosen by the coach.
- Each game lasts 5 minutes.
- The period between games is 1 minute.
- 3 points are awarded for a goal and 1 point for a draw.

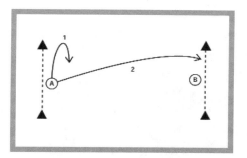

Game "From goal to goal after a throw"

- Two goals are set up 4 to 7 yards apart.
- Player A throws the ball from the goal line to B
- B tries to head the ball into the goal and score a point.
- The height of the goal is the height of the players.

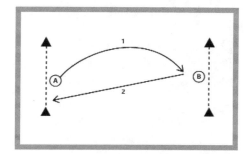

Note
- The thrower must throw the ball in such a way that the opponent can head it easily.
- If the ball is thrown inaccurately, the opponent can catch it and throw it back.

Game: Handball - headers (4 against 4)
Rules as in the previous practice session. This time the ball must be headed after each third pass at the latest. After each header the players restart with the "one."

Variations for more advanced players
The ball is played from one player to the other with a drop-kick or drop-volley. If the ball falls to the ground, possession goes to the other team.

E) End game
Game of 8 against 8. Headed goals count for 5 points, thus providing an incentive for playing down the wings and crossing the ball to create openings for headers.

Series 6: Shooting at goal

The favorite shooting drill of many coaches of young soccer players is as follows. The coach stands level with the edge of the penalty area and 16 young players stand in a line 10 to 15 yards away. The first player passes to the coach, who passes the back diagonally for the player to run onto and shoot. Each player probably has, at most, 3 or 4 shots at goal. Unfortunately such ineffective drills are encountered far too often. The young players learn slowly and have too little movement. Only one person is fully involved, and that is the coach.

Effective coaching for shooting at goal should satisfy the following criteria:

- There must be lots of repetitions and intensive drills to give the young players sufficient opportunities to improve their shooting technique. For this reason, shooting drills should make use of as many goals as possible, preferably with nets.
- Once the basic skills have been dealt with, the drills should simulate game situations as closely as possible.
- The coach must pay attention to correct posture (upper body, position of the feet, backlift) and tactical errors (position relative to the ball, running paths, variations in pace).

PRACTICE SESSION S I
BASIC DRILLS

In this first session the players learn the basic techniques for shooting hard at goal. The coach should correct mistakes at once. In particular, the standing foot should be positioned about one foot-width from the ball, i.e. not too far away from it, and should point in the shooting direction. The front of the shooting foot should point slightly downward. To impart maximum acceleration to the ball, the leg must be bent during the backlift and straightened just before it comes into contact with the ball.

A) Setting the mood
- Small sided game W11 - Target shooting

B) Warm-up drill
Directional dribbling

C) Coordination conditioning
Drills with the coordination ladder and a ball.

D) Main phase: Basic shooting drills
Shooting at a goal in groups of 3

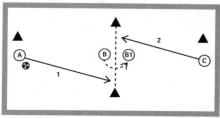

- The 2 outside players take turns at shooting the stationary ball at the goal in the middle (size: 3 - 5 yards).
- The distance of the players from the goal is 8 - 12 yards, depending on the players age, strength, etc.
- The goalkeeper turns to face each player in turn before they shoot.

- If the ball rebounds from the goalkeeper, the player tries to score from the rebound.
- After 10 shots the players swap roles. Each player takes one turn in the goal.
- The winner is the player who shoots the most goals.

First-time shot after pass into the player's path
The coach selects a zone where the ball will be stopped by a fence or a net, so that the players do not have to run far to fetch the ball after a shot.

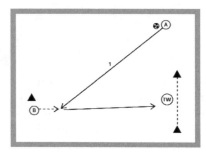

A) Pass from the goal line - shot on the run
- Player A pushes the ball into the path of B, who is behind the shooting line at a distance of 10 yards from the goal.
- A goalkeeper is in the goal.
- The shooter can try to score from rebounds.
- All the balls are played back to A.
- After 10 shots the players swap roles.
- The player who scores the most goals is the winner.

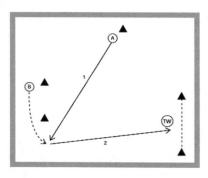

B) Pass from the side - shot on the turn

C) Pass from behind - shot after taking the ball and turning with it

- Beginners should learn how to take a pass and run with the ball at an early stage. They can also do this in the context of shooting at goal.

- Modern soccer is very fast. To accustom the players to this, only three ball contacts are allowed: first touch (control), second touch (push the ball into a shooting position) and shot.

- The players can take the ball and push it with the inside or outside of the foot in combination with a turn.

- From the very beginning, the coach should always encourage the players to practice using both feet.

Shot after a short sprint to the ball

- Player A pushes the ball into space and player B1 sprints toward it.
- B1 tries to shoot into the goal.
- After the shot, B1 fetches the ball and goes to A's position.

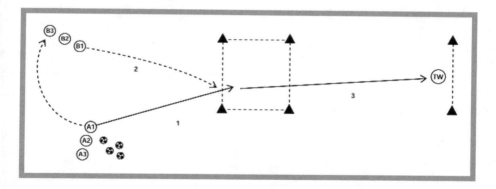

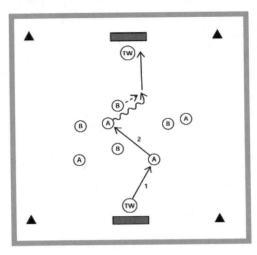

E) End game: 4 against 4 with 2 goals and 2 goalkeepers

Two goals (preferably with nets) are set up 20 yards apart. In a small area 2 teams play 4 against 4 (or 5 against 5) and try to score goals as quickly as possible. The players can shoot from any distance. The defenders are thus forced to challenge quickly before players shoot from distance. If only 2 goals are available, the other players should play in a second area. The players can switch from one area to the other at agreed intervals.

PRACTICE SESSION S 2
SHOT AFTER A DRIBBLE

To coach players effectively in how to shoot, a competitive element must be introduced. For this reason shots at goal should be incorporated into practice drills that enable the player to shoot at goal in situations that resemble a real game. It is therefore essential that players shoot while on the move within complex situations. The coach starts with simple passing sequences followed by a shot, and builds up to more difficult combinations involving opponents, so that the players have to react quickly under pressure from opponents. Shots at goal after a dribble should also be included.

A) Setting the mood
Warm-up game: G11 - Pickpocket and/or G16 - Dribbling through the goal

B) Warm-up drill
Repetition of the give-and-go with a wall player.

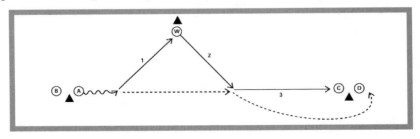

C) Coordination conditioning
Drills with the coordination ladder followed by a task (passing game at the end).

D) Main phase
Dribbling and shot at goal (with opponent)
The first player in each line (A1, B1) runs with the ball toward the opponent in the marked square, dribbles round him/her, and shoots at goal. At first the opponent should challenge only half-heartedly and allow the attacker to trick him. Only when the attackers are strong enough do the defenders challenge wholeheartedly. At this stage the attackers can compete with the defenders. A successful dribble scores one point and 2 awarded for a goal.
Organization: After shooting, the attackers take the ball and join the end of the other group.

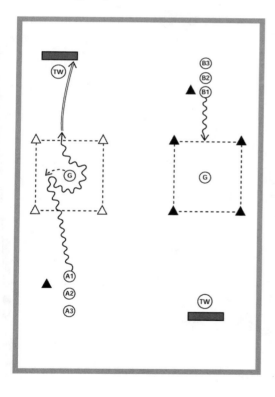

Dribbling + shot at goal (against 2 defenders)

The players are under more pressure if they have to dribble past 2 defenders before shooting at goal.

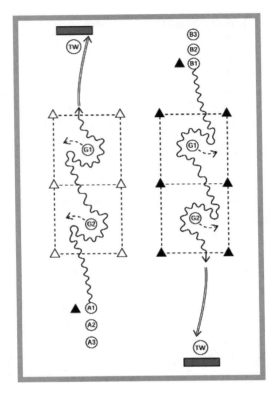

Takeover

A line of players stands at each of 2 corners of the penalty area. One group has a ball and the other does not. B glances at A and then starts to dribble toward A, while A runs toward B. In the middle A takes the ball over from B, dribbles toward the goal and finishes with a shot. Both players subsequently join the end of the opposite lines (A fetches the ball).

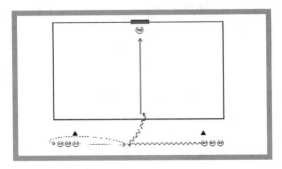

Dribble + shot at goal after
takeover, with defender
In this drill the defender runs parallel to the attacker and blocks
his/her path to the goal. A takes
over the ball on the side furthest
away from goal, dribbles toward the
goal and shoots. A second defender
waits in readiness, so that the next
pair of players can start. The first
defender runs back to group B.

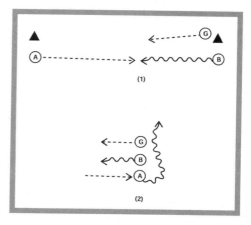

PRACTICE SESSION S 3
SHOT AT GOAL AFTER GIVE-AND-GO

A) Setting the mood
Warm-up game: G3 - Grand prix and/or G12 - Six-day race

B) Warm-up drill
Repetition of taking the ball and running backward with it.

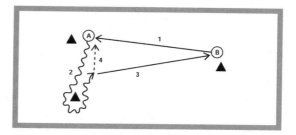

C) Coordination conditioning
Drills with the coordination ladder (arranged in a right angle).

Main phase: Shot at goal after a passing combination
Shot at goal and additional task
The attacker (A1) plays a give-and-go with B1, shoots at goal (from 15
yards) and sprints to the coach, who plays or throws a second ball to
him/her. The second task could be, for example, a shot at goal from a short
distance or a header from a throw

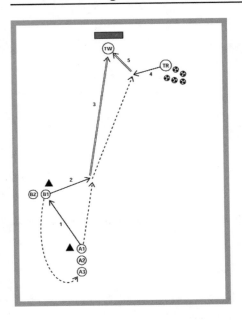

The attacker A1 plays one ball to the coach and another ball to the wall player B1. After shooting, A1 joins the wall players. B1 joins the attackers. In this way the players continuously swap roles.

Shot at goal after 2 give-and gos

The attacker (A1) plays 2 give-and-gos with wall players W1 and W2 and then shoots at goal. The wall players swap positions at regular intervals with the attackers.

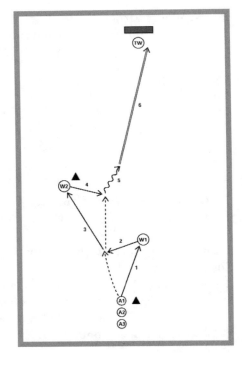

Shooting competition

A(1) plays a long ball to A(2), who plays the ball back diagonally to him/her. A(1) sprints onto the ball ands plays it into the path of A(2). A(2) shoots. B(1) now plays a long ball to B(2). Each goal is counted. The team to score 10 goals first is the winner. Alternatively, the team that scores the most goals in 10 minutes is the winner.

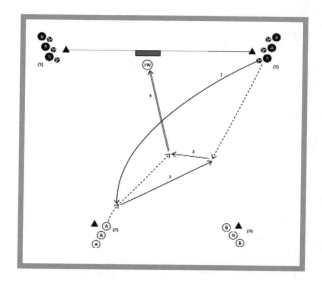

E) End game

• Burnout
• Game with 2 big goals. Goals scored from outside the shooting zone count double (reward for long shots).

PRACTICE SESSION S 4
SHOT AT GOAL AFTER A PASSING COMBINATION

A) Setting the tone
Warm-up games: G8 - Island hopping and/or G10 - Shield the ball

B) Warm-up drill
Give-and-go with two wall players (W)

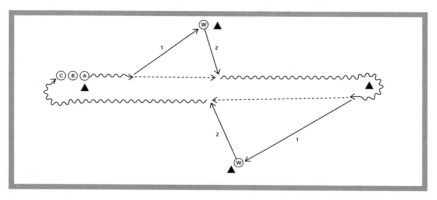

C) Coordination conditioning
Coordination conditioning with shot at goal.

D) Main phase: Shooting at goal for more advanced players
Combination drill 1:

A passes to B, who plays the ball into the path of A, who plays the ball into the path of B, who sprints to the ball and shoots at the goal. A joins the end of group B. B fetches the ball and joins the end of group A.

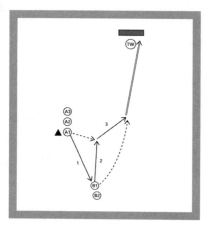

Combination drill 2

A1 plays a give-and-go with B, plays the ball to C and takes over B's position. B sprints to position C after the give-and-go and waits for the next pass. C plays the ball into the path of D, who runs onto it and shoots. D fetches the ball and joins the back of group A.

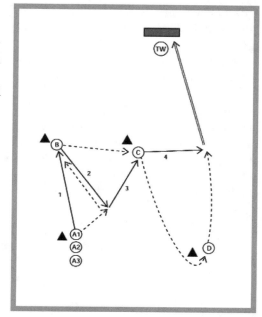

Combination drill 3

A1 plays a give-and-go with B and passes immediately to C. C plays the ball into the path of B, who runs round the cone and shoots on the run. A1 takes over the position of B. B fetches the ball and gives it to C, who joins the back of group A.

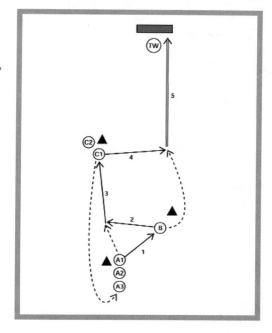

Combination drill 4

A1 plays the ball to B, who runs a few steps toward it and plays it back to A1. A1 plays the returned ball diagonally to C, who plays it straight across the playing area to B. B plays the ball into the path of C, who controls it and shoots at the goal. Each player then moves round one position (A to B, B to C, C fetches the ball and joins the back of group A).

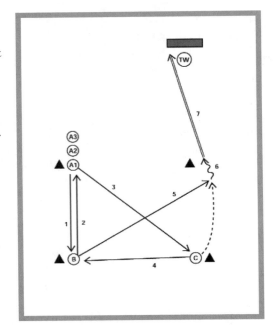

E) End: Lightning tournament

The lightning tournament encourages fast build-up play and finishing. The rules virtually exclude players from keeping the ball and slowing the game down, as both teams lose if no goals are scored in the agreed time. Lightning tournaments are thus very dynamic.

Tournament rules

- The players are divided into groups of 3 or 4.
- Teams A and B start the first game and the other teams (C, D, E, etc.) wait in a file. When a team loses it joins the back of the file.
- Both teams try to score within an agreed time (1 or 2 minutes). The team that succeeds stays on the field and the other joins the back of the file. The first team in the file takes its place.
- If neither team scores, both teams join the back of the file and the first 2 teams in the file take their place.
- The team with the most points, i.e. the most wins, is the tournament winner.

Tip

- The coach can single out the team with the longest series of wins for special praise.

Indoor coaching sessions

Indoor coaching is not popular with many coaches of young soccer players. Even during the winter months they prefer to stage practice sessions out-doors. Such coaches justify this by referring to the problems that can arise when large groups practice in small indoor facilities. They see few options for planning and implementing targeted soccer coaching, as frequently only a small hall is available for a large numbers of players. Practice sessions are then often limited to games in which few players can participate and the rest can only watch.

Indoor coaching has some organizational and methodic advantages Alongside the independence of wind and weather, indoor coaching offers a number of advantages and can be a meaningful extension of outdoor coach-ing. The conditions indoors (playing area, walls, equipment, etc.) can be inte-grated into the drills.

PRACTICE SESSION I I
GAMES

A) Setting the mood
Warm-up game: G13 - 100-points dribbling
This game is especially suitable for indoor coaching. The use of music can also help to set the mood.

B) Warm-up drill
Continuous formats are useful where space is restricted. This drill allows the players to practice passing with the inside of the foot (one or two contacts), headers, throwing and catching, drop-kick and catching, etc.

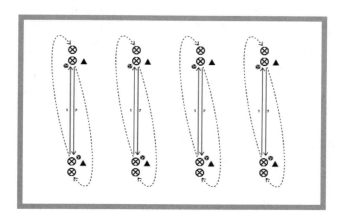

C) Coordination conditioning

Tires are available in most indoor facilities. These can be used for jumping-jack coordination sequences. Such a sequence can be finished off by throwing and heading a ball.

D) Main phase: Small sided games

The following games make excellent use of the available space and enable a lot of players to participate. The focus is on improving soccer techniques.
• Hit the cones (see pp. 57, 58)
• Billiard soccer (see pp. 57)
• Indoor flatball (see pp. 60, 61)

E) End game

Game I6 - Zone soccer (see pp. 61,62)

PRACTICE SESSION I 2
INTERVAL TRAINING

The second indoor practice session is aimed at older players, who can go round a course carrying out a series of drills at various stopping points ("stations") as quickly as possible. The emphasis is on using soccer techniques (passing, heading, shooting, taking a pass and running with the ball) at intervals. The rest periods while the players proceed from one station to the next should not exceed 1 minute. The phases of this practice session are the same as for all other sessions. A warm-up game to set the mood is followed by a warm-up drill to improve coordination. After the main phase this session ends with a lightning tournament.

Using the walls

The walls of the hall are an ideal aid for goalkeepers and field players. They can be used to practice key aspects of ball control and to develop a feel for the ball as well as fast reactions. Gymnastic benches (turned on their side), box upper sections, small boxes, etc. can be used to create other variations. Some of the players can aim at a target at waist height or higher on the wall while the others aim at a low target on a small box, a turned-over bench, etc. After an agreed time the groups can swap places.

A) Setting the mood

Warm-up game: G8 - Island hopping
Hoops or small boxes or mats can serve as islands.

B) Warm-up drill
An indoor floor is ideal for drills one-touch low passing.

C) Coordination
Fast foot movements with the coordination ladder

D) Main phase - Interval training
The organization aspects are kept as simple as possible. The players move in a group from one station to the next, but each player has an individual task to carry out with the ball.

Station 1: Dribbling, passing, taking a pass and running with the ball
The players dribble toward a wall. Two or three yards from the wall they play the ball against the wall, take the rebound with the inside or outside of the foot and dribble round their cone. If the wall is not suitable (e.g. large base boards), small boxes or turned-over benches can be used.

Station 2: Drop-volley against the wall, taking the rebound on the chest
This drill requires a flat wall, from which the ball will rebound normally. Beginners can throw the ball against the wall and take the rebound on the chest.
(Variation: Control the rebound with the head or thigh)

Station 3: Dribbling in comb pattern with shot at goal
The comb (see pp. 118, 119) is ideal for indoor practice sessions, as it allows many players to be involved at the same time. In this practice session the comb is combined with a shot at goal. The players then dribble back round the comb to the starting point. A goalkeeper is not essential but can be involved if desired. The gaps between dribblers should not be too short, as the players should be able to shoot as they finish the dribble and not have to wait while the previous player fetches his/her ball out of the goal.

Station 4: Rebound passing
The players kick the ball repeatedly against the wall using the inside of the foot or the instep, using the right and the left foot, gradually moving closer to the wall so that they have to react more quickly.

Station 5: Dribbling in a zigzag followed by a shot at goal

This drill is similar to the drill at station 3 (comb). The players dribble around a zigzag course and then shoot at goal. They retrieve the ball and then dribble back round the zigzag.

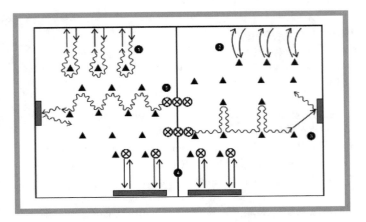

E) End game

- Game W16 - Kings and soldiers (see pp. 67-69).
- 2 against 2 with 4 neutral outside players

The 2 players of team A play against the 2 players of team B. They can involve the neutral players, who are allowed only one or two ball contacts each time they receive the ball. After 1 or 2 minutes the players swap roles. Teams A and B take over from the neutral players, who split up into 2 teams.

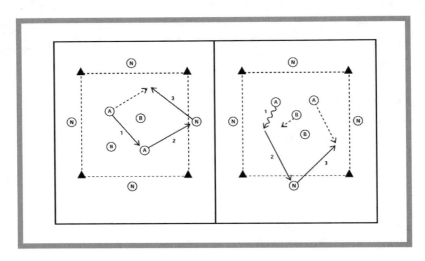

Final comments

At this point I would like to emphasize that this book is not intended to cover all aspects of soccer and to include practice sessions for all possible themes. On grounds of size alone, it can only contain a number of selected examples described in as much detail as necessary. I hope that this book inspires coaches to develop their own drills based on those described here. The content of the practice sessions and the games can be variably combined to suit the age and skill levels of young players. Try it.

This book is aimed at coaches who are always on the lookout for new drills and games to try out with their players. I wish all readers lots of enjoyment and success in trying out, using, varying and combining these drills.

Peter Schreiner

The author

Peter Schreiner

- Sports instructor and A-license coach with many years of experience in youth and amateur soccer in Germany (e.g. Schalke 04 under-18s and division 1 of German amateur league)
- Coaching instructor and lecturer at national and international soccer education events
- Lecturer at sports instructor courses
- Author of more than ten soccer coaching videos and numerous contributions to journals
- Head of the Institut für Jugendfussball (Institute for Youth Soccer)
- Co-founder of the Deutsche Fussball-Akademie (German Soccer Academy)

Other Peter Schreiner Titles Available from Reedswain:

BOOKS

Item 265
Coordination, Agility and Speed Training For Soccer
$14.95

Item 266
24 Easy to Follow Practice Sessions for 5-7 Year Olds
$12.95

Item 297
24 Easy to Follow Practice Sessions for 8-11 Year Olds
$12.95

Item 256
The Creative Dribbler
$14.95

www.reedswain.com
800-331-5191

Other Peter Schreiner Titles Available from Reedswain:

VIDEOS/DVDs

Item 769
Coordination and Agility Training with a Ball
$29.95
Available on VHS or DVD

Item 900
Soccerobics
$29.95

Item 138
The German Touch
Set of 3 Videos
$79.95

Item 228
Coordination, Agility and Speed
Training for Soccer
Set of 2 Videos or 1 DVD
$49.95

www.reedswain.com
800-331-5191

Equipment Used in this Book Available from Reedswain

Disc Cone Hurdles

Visit us online at
www.reedswain.com
or call
800-331-5191
for a free catalog of soccer books,
videos/dvd, software and
equipment

Agility Poles

Tall Cones

Coordination Ladder

Disc Cones